COMMUNICATION IN ORGANIZATIONS

Author: Corinne Leech

Series Editor: Kate Williams

ELSEVIER

Pergamon
Flexible
Learning

AMSTERDAM • BOSTON • HEIDELBERG • LONDON • OXFORD • NEW YORK • PARIS • SAN DIEGO • SAN FRANCISCO • SINGAPORE • SYDNEY • TOKYO

Elsevier
Linacre House, Jordan Hill, Oxford OX2 8DP
30 Corporate Drive, Burlington, MA 01803

First published 2005

British Library Cataloguing in Publication Data
Leech, Corinne
   Communication in organizations – (Chartered Management
   Institute's open learning programme)
   1. Communication in management
   I. Title   II Chartered Management Institute
   658.4'5

ISBN 0 7506 6428 2

For information on all Elsevier publications visit our website at
http://books.elsevier.com

Typeset by Charon Tec Pvt. Ltd, Chennai, India
Printed and bound in Italy

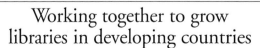

Communication in Organizations

Chartered Management Institute Open Learning Programme

OTHER BOOKS WITHIN THIS SERIES

Contents

Series overview

The Chartered Management Institute Flexible Learning programme is a series of workbooks prepared by the Chartered Management Institute and Elsevier for managers seeking to develop themselves.

Comprising ten open learning workbooks, the programme covers the best of modern management theory and practice. Each workbook provides a range of frameworks and techniques to improve your effectiveness as a manager, thus helping you to acquire the knowledge and skill to make you fully competent in your role.

Each workbook is written by an experienced management writer and covers an important management topic or theme. The activities both reinforce learning and help to relate the generic ideas to your individual work context. While coverage of each topic is fully comprehensive, additional reading suggestions and reference sources are given for those who wish to study in greater depth.

Designed to be practical, stimulating and challenging, the aim of the workbooks is to improve performance at work by benefiting you and your organization. This practical focus is at the heart of the competence-based approach that has been adopted by the programme.

Introduction

Effective communication lies at the heart of all successful organizations. People have to communicate to make anything happen. For example, you need to communicate to:

- develop relationships
- motivate your team
- make presentations
- negotiate
- instruct and inform
- participate in meetings.

Generally, people's preferred method of communication is face to face. If you work in close proximity to your team then it's likely that face-to-face conversations are the dominant method of communication with your team. Dispersed teams will rely more heavily on telephone and e-mail. However, as you move out of your team it's more likely that methods of communication fall into the 'written' category, e.g. reports, e-mails, letters, etc.

The process of communication is relatively straightforward and can be represented in five steps:

1. 'Sender' has something to communicate
↓
2. Translates into words
↓
3. Sends message
↓
4. 'Receiver' hears/reads words
↓
5. Interprets what sender intended to communicate

But getting communication to work in organizations is a huge challenge.

Two-thirds of American workers say that poor communication prevents them from doing their best work

(Poor Communications, *Newsweek*, 12, August 1996)

So why does a relatively straightforward process cause so much difficulty? To find the answer, you have to look at all the factors which affect the process, rather than just the process itself. For example:

- the *culture* of an organization will set the scene for what's communicated by the organization and how it's received by employees
- the *relationship* you have with your team will influence what you communicate and how it's received by individual members of the team
- your *mood* at a particular time influences what your body language communicates to anyone you meet
- your *feelings, beliefs and values* will impact on what you decide to communicate and the interpretation you put on what you hear.

Therefore, becoming more effective at communicating is about becoming more skilled at the process *and* more sensitive to the context.

Skilled at process + sensitive to context = better at communicating

This workbook looks at issues relating to both the process and the context. You will find a number of activities which will ask you to reflect on the communication aspects of recent situations and identify learning points. The most powerful way to develop your communication skills is to get into the mindset of consciously applying the cycle of:

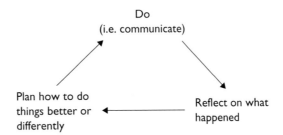

It's a process everyone uses throughout their life to a greater or lesser degree. However, if you get into the habit of consciously reflecting on things, then you learn and develop much more effectively. It's not an onerous task; all that's involved is getting into the mindset of thinking about what's going on around you.

Objectives

By the end of this workbook, you should be better able to:

- reflect on the messages you send when you communicate
- listen effectively
- check that what you communicate has been understood
- understand factors which underpin the communications' process
- plan and reflect on the way you communicate whenever you interact with people
- manage meetings effectively
- write in plain English
- structure a report.

Section 1 Communicating: analysing the process

Introduction

Our communication skills are something we tend to take for granted. Of course we're all skilled at communicating; it's something we've been doing since the day we were born. We communicate spontaneously, often unconsciously, and sometimes find that we have to live with the consequences.

People react to your behaviour, i.e. what you do and say. It's the only clue they have to interpret the complex nature of what goes on inside your head:

There are four ways, and only four ways, in which we have contact with the world. We are evaluated and classified by these contacts: what we do, how we look, what we say and how we say it.

Dale Carnegie

Having a greater insight into what's happening when you communicate increases your ability to adapt the way you interact with people and influence their response to you. Increasing your awareness of the process and context of communication will increase your effectiveness of working with others.

The communication process

The first model of the communication process was developed by Claude Shannon and Warren Weaver in 1949. The aim of the model was to enable engineers from the Bell Telephone Company to transmit mechanical messages more effectively (Figure 1.1).

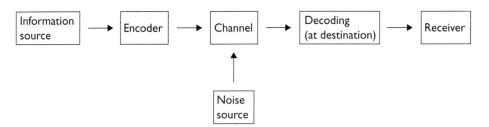

Figure 1.1 Shannon and Weaver Model of Communication. (*Source*: adapted from Shannon, C. and Weaver, W. (1963) *The Mathematical Theory of Communication*, University of Illinois Press.)

Although developed for mechanical messages, the model successfully captures what happens when people communicate and provides a starting point for understanding what's happening when we communicate. For example:

Shannon–Weaver element	Equivalent in human communication
Source	Sender is the person who sends the message
Encoder	Sender chooses the words for the message
Channel	This could be face to face, e-mail, written
Receiver	This is the person who will receive the message
Decoding	The receiver of the message has to interpret the message and understand it
Noise source	Anything that interferes with the message being received by the receiver

Breaking down the communication process into these stages can be used for pinpointing where pitfalls can occur when people communicate. For example, you may choose words which are confusing or over-complicated (i.e. message fails at the encoding stage). Alternatively, the person you talk to may not be listening or have the knowledge to interpret your words (decoding faulty) or the message may never get to the intended person (channel failure).

ACTIVITY 1

Identify instances when something you communicated failed, or partly failed, because of problems in each of the following areas.

Examples of communication failure due to:

Encoding:

Channel:

Decoding:

FEEDBACK

Although mechanistic, briefly stopping to consider the process of communication and potential for problems can be helpful in preventing a communication failure. We'll look at these areas in more detail in the context of verbal communication.

Encoding the message

Most people focus on selecting the words to convey a message. In fact it's even more important to be aware of the messages that your body language and tone are giving as psychologists claim that over half the message you convey comes from non-verbal messages. For example, Mehrabian[1] deduced that:

- 55 per cent is based on your body language
- 38 per cent on the way you say something
- 7 per cent on the words you use.

We'll explore these three components of verbal communication in turn.

BODY LANGUAGE

Non-verbal communication covers all the ways in which we send messages to people when interacting with them that does not involve the use of words. It includes:

- **Facial expressions**   These reflect what a person is feeling, e.g. interest, surprise and fear. They can often override the message sent in words. For example, a person may hear 'pleased to see you', but a momentary frown might have sent a clear message that they weren't pleased to see you at all. Most facial expressions are the same across all cultures; they are innate and shared by all human beings. For example, the spontaneous facial expressions which denote fear, joy, sadness or excitement:

  Eyebrows are important in the expressing of emotions. Perhaps most important is the 'eyebrow flash', a rapid up and down flick of the eyebrows that conveys recognition and approval. The ability to telegraph friendly intentions from a safe distance would have had obvious survival value for our ancestors.[2]

- **Eye contact**   This plays an important part in verbal communication. Generally, people who like each other have more eye contact than people who don't; you search for more eye contact when you listen than when you speak. The amount of eye contact varies between cultures. For example, people from 'contact cultures', e.g. South Americans, or those from the Mediterranean area, tend to engage in more eye contact than people from non-contact cultures, e.g. North Europeans and Asians.

- **Posture and gestures**   These include the way we stand, sit and move. They can give strong messages about what a person is feeling. For example, arms crossed can mean a person is feeling defensive or unsure; covering your mouth can indicate lack of confidence, drumming fingers indicates impatience. People who are deeply engrossed in discussion will mirror each other's body language. A mirroring body will often help to create rapport, e.g. if someone leans forward the other person will also lean forward.

- **Use of space and touch**   This is influenced by cultural rules. For example, some cultures, e.g. contact cultures, readily integrate the use of touch, whereas other cultures are less tactile, e.g. non-contact cultures. People from contact cultures stand or sit closer to each other than non-contact cultures.

A study by Jourard[3] showed how many times couples touched each other in cafes in different parts of the world:

- Puerto Rico: 180 times per hour
- Paris: 110 times per hour
- London: 0 times per hour.

Research by Gudykunst[4] showed that people behave differently when they interact with people who they perceive as being culturally different to those who they perceive as being culturally the same and concluded that people find it much easier to get to know people from similar cultures.

Body language is very difficult to control. Some experts believe it's impossible to fake it, whereas others argue that you can control up to 15 per cent. Whatever it is in practice it's useful to be aware that:

- your body language will be sending messages every time you interact with other people
- the more you tune-in to other people's body language, the more effective you can become in interpersonal relationships.

People vary in their ability to pick up cues from body language. Some people are very sensitive to the body language of others, and will interpret and respond to it spontaneously; others can be almost immune and completely switch off from picking up on any non-verbal messages. It's beyond the scope of this workbook to explore the reasons for this. However, it is becoming clear that people who have highly developed skills of interacting with people are the ones likely to become most successful in today's workplace:

The rules for work are changing. We're being judged by a new yardstick: not just by how smart we are, or by our training and expertise, but also by how well we handle ourselves and each other... These rules have little to do with what we were told was important in school; academic abilities are largely irrelevant to this standard. The new measure takes for granted having enough intellectual ability and technical know-how to do our jobs; it focuses instead on personal qualities, such as initiative and empathy, adaptability and persuasiveness.

Goleman[5]

Goleman also cites a study of top executives at 15 global companies, including Pepsi, Volvo and IBM, and concludes that success at the highest levels could be attributed to 90 per cent emotional intelligence, and the remaining 10 per cent to technical and intellectual competence.

ACTIVITY 2

Identify two recent occasions when you picked up cues from the body language of people at work. For each one identify how your interpretation of the body language influenced your response in the situation.

Incident 1:

Incident 2:

FEEDBACK

The ease with which you completed this activity is likely to be a measure of how tuned-in and sensitive you are to the non-verbal messages sent by others. Becoming more aware of body language involves consciously looking for clues as you interact with people. As you tune-in to the body language you'll find you'll be able to instinctively respond to it. Where appropriate, try shutting your eyes when you talk to someone. You'll notice just how much you rely on non-verbal signals as you talk.

THE WAY YOU SAY IT

We convey a lot through the way we say things. The pitch of our voice, rate of speech and loudness all combine to convey meaning. A person can use exactly the same words when answering a phone on two occasions but convey completely different meanings depending on the emphasis placed on different words.

Generally, the way you are feeling will be conveyed in your voice. Most people will automatically rely on the message conveyed by *how* you say something rather than what you say.

THE WORDS YOU CHOOSE

Most of the time we speak spontaneously; often not knowing which words we're going to use until they're spoken. However, at work you often need to think through the main points you want to make to:

- give structure to what you say
- make sure you include all the points you want to make.

It's also important not to introduce over-complicated language or jargon into what you say. It will result in communication failure as the receiver struggles to decode the message.

Your choice of words can also encourage particular responses. Honey[6] identified nine main types of verbal behaviour:

- **Seeking ideas**   Asking someone else for their ideas or opinions
  - What do you think?
  - Do you think it will work?
- **Proposing**   Putting forward a definite plan or idea
  - Shall we … ?
  - I think the best plan of action is …
- **Suggesting**   Tentatively putting forward an idea or plan
  - What about … ?
  - Maybe we could …
- **Building**   This involves building on another person's ideas or suggestions
  - We could then …
  - What about then using the results to … ?
- **Disagreeing**   Clearly disagreeing with what someone has said
  - I don't think that will work
  - That's not the case.
- **Supporting**   Agreeing with what someone says
  - I can see that working
  - That's a good idea.
- **Difficulty stating**   Pointing out any potential difficulties
  - But what if … ?
  - That won't work because …
- **Clarifying/explaining/informing**   Providing factual information
  - It means that …
  - The plan is to …
- **Seeking clarification/information**   Asking for more information
  - What would the implications be?
  - How do you … ?

For each type of behaviour he calculated the likelihood of particular responding types of behaviour. For example:

■ If you 'seek ideas' it has a:
  – 60 per cent likelihood of someone proposing in response
  – 19 per cent likelihood of someone suggesting in response.
■ If you 'propose' it has a:
  – 39 per cent likelihood of someone having difficulty stating in response
  – 25 per cent likelihood of someone supporting in response.
■ If you make a 'suggestion' it has a:
  – 42 per cent chance of someone supporting in response
  – 18 per cent chance of someone having difficulty stating in response
  – 17 per cent chance of someone seeking clarification/information in response.

Whilst there's no need to learn the percentage likelihood of responses it's useful to recognize that:

■ other people's responses aren't completely random
■ your verbal behaviour can shape their response.

The more aware and sensitive you can become to how other people react, the more you'll be able to steer the response you get from others.

CHOOSING THE CHANNEL

How are you going to send the message? There may be a choice and you need to consider the most appropriate channel from the receiver's point of view.

Verbal (if so when and where)

■ One to one
■ Group
■ Presentation
■ Formally
■ Informally
■ Phone.

Written

■ E-mail message
■ E-mail and attachment
■ Print
■ Noticeboard
■ Publication, e.g. newsletter.

Using Shannon and Weaver's terminology, there are a number of 'noise sources' which can affect the channel and cause the message to fail to reach the sender or become distorted. For example, if you decide to use the phone, will the absence of body language distort the message? Is it the wrong environment to discuss an issue in the canteen? In the case of written communication, how do you make sure that the receiver will actually get the document to read in the required timescale?

ACTIVITY 3

Consider your response in Activity 1 related to the channel. How could the problem over the channel have been avoided?

FEEDBACK

Often the success of a channel is bound up with how the receiver responds. The channel as a means may have worked but it also has to sufficiently motivate the receiver to decode the message.

Decoding the message

ACTIVITY 4

Who has responsibility for decoding the message:

- ❑ the receiver?
- ❑ the sender?
- ❑ both?

FEEDBACK

Responsibility has to lie with the receiver; they have to decode the message and make sense of it. However, there's a common belief that if you send information to someone, you have communicated. For example:

I told them all about it during the site meeting, including what to do if they had concerns. It's no good introducing problems at this late stage.

Or in the case of written information:

I will send the e-mail with the customer feedback report attached and ask for comments by 26th. If I don't hear anything by then I assume they've got no comments so we'll go ahead with the recommendations.

The act of sending information doesn't automatically shift responsibility onto the receiver for making sense of information. First the sender has to make sure that the receivers are actively engaged with the communication process; only then can responsibility shift to the receiver to interpret the information.

ACTIVITY 5

Identify an occasion when you failed to communicate because the receiver didn't engage and attempt to understand your message. Identify the reasons for this happening and how you could have behaved differently to ensure that the message was received.

When did it happen?	Why did it happen?	What could you have done differently?

FEEDBACK

Get into the habit of thinking that you, as a sender, are responsible for getting your message across. It will help you tailor what and how you communicate to the receiver, and make you a more effective communicator.

In verbal communication, the receiver's role is to listen. Listening to someone sends a powerful message that you value them. Implicit in listening is the message 'you're worth devoting my time to; what you have to say is important'. It can effectively build up someone's self-esteem. In contrast, paying lip service to listening will soon send a loud and clear message that you do not value the other person. Listening enables you to understand another person's point of view. Covey stresses the importance of understanding in his book:

If I were to summarise in one sentence the single most important principle I have learned in the field of interpersonal relations, it would be this: Seek first to understand, then to be understood.[7]

Being able to listen is the key to effective communication.

Effective listening

People can speak at approximately 160 words a minute; our brains can think at equivalent to 1000 words a minute.

ACTIVITY 6

What implication does this have for listening?

FEEDBACK

It's very easy to listen half-heartedly. Our minds can be doing anything from formulating responses to thinking about something completely different as we appear to be listening. There are many reasons why we don't listen to someone who is talking.

Nine reasons for not listening

1   I don't need to hear what you've got to say; I know it already.
2   I don't want to hear what you've got to say; it might embarrass me.
3   I don't care what you say, so I'm thinking about my reply.
4   I don't want to listen to you because I don't like you.
5   I'm getting bored because you're taking too long to make your point.
6   I'm getting confused because you're going too fast for me.
7   I've got more important things on my mind right now.
8   I'm more interested in what is going on over there.
9   I'm in a hurry, and if I show interest you might keep me here longer.

Source: adapted from Reilly, P. (1993) *The Skills Development Book for Busy Managers*, McGraw-Hill.

ACTIVITY 7

What behaviours (verbal and non-verbal) convey that someone is not listening?

FEEDBACK

Behaviours include lack of sufficient eye contact, a glazed expression, interrupting, not being able to reply to questions, turning their body away, showing impatience. In practice it's quite difficult to carry on talking when someone is clearly not listening.

Listening is not the same as hearing. Hearing is a passive activity – we can hear something without actually processing the information. Listening involves making sense of what we hear. It's an active process which demands complete attention.

How to listen

1   Stop talking. You can't listen if you are talking.
2   Imagine the other person's viewpoint.
3   Look, act and **be** interested.
4   Observe non-verbal behaviour.
5   Don't interrupt.
6   Listen between the lines for things left unsaid or unexplained. Ask about them.
7   Make no judgment or criticism when listening.
8   Rephrase and reflect back what the other person has said at key points of the conversation to check understanding.
9   Stop talking – this is the first and last, because all other techniques of listening depend on it.

Source: adapted from Senge *et al.* (1994) *The Fifth Discipline Fieldbook*, Nicholas Brearley Publishing Limited.

ACTIVITY 8

Consider the listening checklist above. Which two points in the checklist give conclusive evidence to the sender of the message that you are listening?

FEEDBACK

It's only by questioning anything that's been left unsaid or by reflecting back to check understanding that a receiver gives the sender conclusive proof of listening – note that this involves talking and leads us on to viewing the communication as a two-way rather than simply a one-way process.

ACTIVITY 9

Below are the behaviours associated with effective listening as identified by Goleman.[8] For each one, rate yourself on a scale from 1 (I do this) to 5 (I need to improve in this area).

LISTENING OPENLY AND SENDING CONVINCING MESSAGES

People with this competence:

Rating

- ❏ are effective in give-and-take, registering emotional cues in attuning their message
- ❏ deal with difficult issues straightforwardly
- ❏ listen well, seek mutual understanding and welcome sharing of information fully
- ❏ foster open communication and stay receptive to bad news as well as good.

Now ask a colleague or friend to rate you or discuss your response with someone you trust.

FEEDBACK

Some people develop these competences instinctively; others have to consciously work on them. However, as we highlighted earlier in the section, the rules for work are changing. For example, a study of top executives at 15 global companies, including Pepsi, Volvo and IBM concluded that, success at the highest levels could be attributes to emotional intelligence, and the remaining 10 per cent to technical and intellectual competence.

Communication is a two-way process

The Shannon–Weaver model represents a one-way communication process, which is essentially about information giving. For example, a presentation to a large audience is a prime example of one-way communication. There is little or no facility for the audience to respond (Figure 1.2).

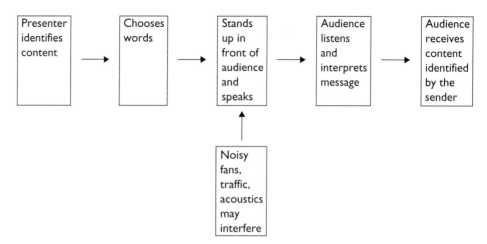

Figure 1.2 *Source:* adapted from Shannon, C. and Weaver, W. (1963) *The Mathematical Theory of Communication,* University of Illinois Press

You can only be sure that communication has taken place if it becomes a two-way process, i.e. feedback from the 'receiver' is returned to the 'sender' to show that the message has been received. So the process of effective communication between people is more accurately represented by Figure 1.3.

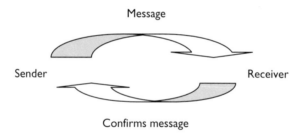

Figure 1.3 Two-way communication process

In face-to-face communication, as dialogue ensues, the roles of sender and receiver become interchangeable as conversation bounces to and fro.

ACTIVITY 10

Consider your experience of the following types of communication. For each one select the response which most accurately describes the process.

	One-way dialogue	Mostly one-way dialogue	Two-way dialogue involving limited feedback	Two-way dialogue
A report you produce for your line manager	❑	❑	❑	❑
Telephone conversation with a customer (internal or external)	❑	❑	❑	❑
Team briefing you give	❑	❑	❑	❑
Team briefing you attend	❑	❑	❑	❑
E-mail you receive from team members	❑	❑	❑	❑
Notice on noticeboard	❑	❑	❑	❑

FEEDBACK

Communicating face to face has the most potential for immediate feedback; but this doesn't necessarily mean that the potential is used or encouraged. Written communication is often one way. Where it is two way, feedback tends to be delayed, although with e-mail, immediate written feedback to the sender is common.

Therefore, communication can be defined as:

A process involving the exchange of information, ideas or feelings between people resulting in a common understanding.

It doesn't have to be two way for communication to take place. However, there is no way of knowing if one-way communication has been effective.

ACTIVITY 11

Consider the definition of communication given above. To what extent do you think it generally describes what happens between members of your team?

Not at all (0%)	Totally (100%)

FEEDBACK

Effective communication results in common understanding. There are times when one-way communication may be more appropriate or when minimum feedback is called for. The acid test is whether or not common understanding has been reached. As we'll see in the next section, there are many factors beyond the process which can affect that understanding.

Learning summary

- People react to your behaviour, i.e. what you do and say. It's the only clue they have to interpret the complex nature of what goes on inside your head.
- Having a greater insight into how you communicate increases your ability to interact with people and influence their response to you.
- Communication can be represented as a process. The process of communication involves a message being sent from a sender to a receiver via a channel. A sender can only be sure a message has been received if they receive feedback.
- The words you use form only a small part of the message you convey when talking. Over 50 per cent of a message is conveyed through your body language.
- The words you choose can influence the response of the receiver. For example, according to Honey, suggesting rather than proposing gives an increased chance of your audience supporting you.

- When you communicate you have some responsibility to make sure that your message is being received and understood.
- Listening effectively is the key to effective communication. There are lots of excuses for not listening. If you want to build good relationships with people you have to overcome these barriers.
- Effective communication results in common understanding.

Into the workplace

You need to:

- reflect on the messages you send when you communicate (this involves giving it some thinking time)
- listen effectively
- check that what you communicate has been understood.

References

1   Mehrabian, A. (1970) Tactics of Social Influence, Prentice Hall
2   The Last Word, New Scientist, 7 August, 2004
3   Jourard, S.M. (1996) An exploratory study of body accessibility, British Journal of Social and Clinical Psychology, 5, 221–231
4   Gudykunst, W.B. (1983) Similarities and differences in perceptions of initial intra-cultural and intercultural encounters: an exploratory investigation, The Southern Speech Communication Journal, 49, 49–65
5   Goleman D. (1999) Working with Emotional Intelligence, Bloomsbury Publishing, p. 3
6   Honey, P. (2001) Improve your People Skills, Chartered Institute of Personnel and Development
7   Covey, S. (1989) Seven Habits of Highly Effective People, Simon & Schuster, p. 237
8   Goleman, D. (1998) Working With Emotional Intelligence, Bloomsbury Publishing

Section 2 Factors influencing the communication process

Introduction

In Section 1 we looked at communication as a mechanistic process. It's a useful starting point, but in practice the way we communicate is influenced by a whole range of factors which can be summarized into being a combination of:

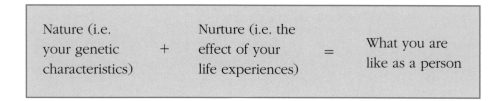

| Nature (i.e. your genetic characteristics) | + | Nurture (i.e. the effect of your life experiences) | = | What you are like as a person |

What you are like as a person influences how you communicate and interpret messages. It underpins the process we explored in Section 1.

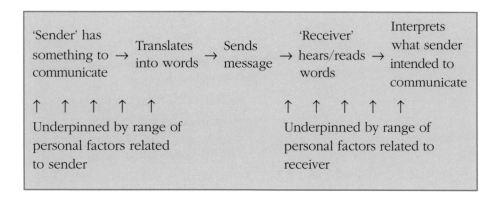

'Sender' has something to communicate → Translates into words → Sends message → 'Receiver' hears/reads words → Interprets what sender intended to communicate

↑ ↑ ↑ ↑ ↑
Underpinned by range of personal factors related to sender

↑ ↑ ↑ ↑ ↑
Underpinned by range of personal factors related to receiver

Your effectiveness as a manager is likely to increase the more you:

■ recognize that there are many factors which affect the communication process
■ become sensitive to the way it affects how you communicate.

In this section we look at some of the theories that contribute towards understanding what makes us tick as people and therefore influence how we communicate. We look briefly at:

■ states of mind
■ being assertive
■ attitudes and assumptions
■ level of trust.

At the end of the section you're asked to review and plan how you communicate drawing on what's been covered in the first two sections.

What's your state of mind?

In the 1950s, Eric Berne developed the theory of 'Transactional Analysis'.[1] He believed that each person's personality is made up of the following states of mind:

■ Adult
■ Parent (learned from their parents or parental substitutes)
■ Child (learned as a child).

During the course of a conversation or 'transaction' everyone has the potential to adopt the corresponding behaviour for the different states of mind.

Behaviours associated with each state of mind are as follows:

You can be in the state of mind of	Associated behaviours
An adult	Thoughtful, making rational judgements and responding accordingly
A parent	Behaviours are associated with either the: ■ **critical parent** opinionated, judgmental, often prejudiced and critical ■ **nurturing parent** caring and protective
A child	Behaviours can result from the: ■ **natural child** direct and spontaneous ■ **manipulative child** hesitant and selfish ■ **adapted child** compliant, apologetic or negative and defiant

ACTIVITY 12

What state of mind is the most conducive to good working relationships?

FEEDBACK

Interactions between 'adult' states give the most effective working relationships. Berne refers to this type of transaction as being 'complementary', i.e. the response follows the pattern of a healthy human relationship. For example:

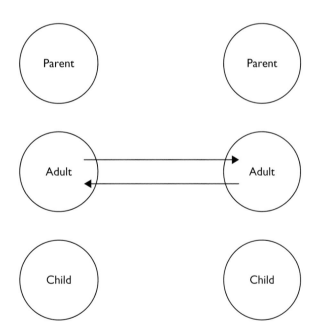

Other types of complementary transactions include parent–parent, or parent–child, which, at times, may play a useful function in the workplace.

Difficulties arise when the states of mind adopted are 'crossed' rather than being complementary.

ACTIVITY 13

Consider the following conversation and identify the states of mind of Kishor and Paul.

	States of mind
Kishor: Can you spare some time later this afternoon to go over the figures? I think we'll have to go right back to the proposal and see where we can cut things out.	
Paul: I've got to go over and see them in finance as well as finish this report. I just can't get my head round looking at that proposal again. Can't it wait?	
Kishor: No, you know what Kevin's like. He'll want to see it first thing in the morning. I'll just have to do it myself.	

FEEDBACK

Kishor seems to start off it a reasonable 'adult' state of mind. Paul responds as a child (adapted) which in turn causes Kishor to respond as a child (manipulative). In a healthy transaction, Paul would have responded as an adult, possibly finding out the reason for the urgency and then at least trying to prioritize to try and make some time. Kishor could have responded as an adult but chose to degenerate into a childish response.

ACTIVITY 14

Spend some time considering the way you interact with different people (at home and work). Can you identify situations when you:

■   Tend to take on the role of a child?

■ Tend to take on the role of a parent (when not in a parental role)?

■ Had to respond to someone who took on the role of child?

■ Had to respond to someone who took on the role of parent?

Which states of mind are you most comfortable:

■ Using?

■ Responding to?

FEEDBACK

Your state of mind will affect the body language you send with any verbal message as well as how you say it. Human conversations are in a constant state of flux, moving between states of minds depending on circumstances. Nobody plays the adult all of the time. Recognizing what's happening in a situation is the first step towards being able to shift the conversation to an adult–adult transaction, or at least ensure that you respond in the adult state. As a manager it's essential that you use the adult ego state in your conversations at work. It's also likely that you'll feel most comfortable with colleagues who also, in the main, use the adult state.

Based on Berne's work, Thomas Harris explored the theory of 'OK life positions'. He identified four main life positions associated with combinations of:

■ OK (feeling good)
■ not OK (feeling bad).

The four main positions were:

■ **I'm OK – You're OK**   This involves feeling positive about yourself and people around you.

■ **I'm OK – You're not OK**   Although individuals feel positive about themselves this is at the expense of feeling superior to others.

■ **I'm not OK – You're OK**   This involves putting yourself down at the expense of feeling that other people are 'better' or superior.

■ **I'm not OK – You're not OK**   Positives are hard to find anywhere with this outlook.

Managers who use the I'm OK – You're OK approach will be able to build more open and trusting relationships at work.

Source: adapted from Harris, T. (2004) *I'm OK – You're OK*, Harpercollins.

Being assertive

Behaviour can be categorized into three types:

■ Assertive behaviour
■ Aggressive behaviour
■ Passive behaviour.

Assertive behaviour is about having the confidence to express your needs, feelings and opinions openly, and respect other people when they express theirs'. Aggressive behaviour is when you put over your needs and feelings at the expense of other people's, and passive behaviour is when you put other people's needs before your own.

Each type of behaviour impacts on the way we communicate.

Communication characteristics of the different type of behaviour		
Aggressive behaviour	**Assertive behaviour**	**Passive behaviour**

■ Forces opinions and ideas on others
■ Often resorts to raising voice or shouts
■ Glare, stare and may use finger pointing
■ Typical types of phrases include:
  – Come on …
  – You'd better …
  – That's stupid
	■ Negotiates and searches for compromises
	■ Keeps true to beliefs and principles
	■ Keeps calm
	■ Comfortable eye contact
	■ Open and relaxed body language
	■ Typical types of phrases include:
	  – I feel …
	  – We could try …
	  – What do you think?
		■ Is overruled by other people's opinions and ideas
		■ Mumbles
		■ Little eye contact
		■ Closed posture – often crossing arms and legs
		■ Typical types of phrases include:
		  – Sorry
		  – I wonder if …
		  – Do you mind if …

ACTIVITY 15

Which of Harris's four main positions would you equate with each of the following behaviour types:

- **Assertive behaviour:**

- **Aggressive behaviour:**

- **Passive behaviour:**

FEEDBACK

Assertive behaviour equates with the I'm OK – You're OK position. Aggressive behaviour is based on I'm OK – You're not OK whereas passive behaviour is the reverse.

The ability to be assertive is related to your self-esteem, i.e. the way you feel about yourself. As with many aspects of personality self-esteem is a result of a complex interaction between your life experiences and your inherited characteristics. Generally, people who receive clear and strong signals throughout their lives that they are valued, liked and loved will, in the main, feel good about themselves and not threatened by other people. Note the addition of the words 'in the main'. Few, if any, people feel good about themselves all of the time. Life tends be like a roller–coaster with ups and downs. Inevitably the 'downs' can dent even the most positive person's self-esteem, if only temporarily.

People who feel good about themselves believe they have certain rights. For example, here are the few rights.

RIGHTS

You have the right to:

- Decide how to lead your life. This includes pursuing your own goals and dreams and establishing your own priorities.
- Your own values, beliefs, opinions and emotions, and the right to respect yourself for them, no matter the opinion of others.
- Not justify or explain your actions or feelings to others.
- Tell others how you wish to be treated.
- Express yourself and to say 'No', 'I don't know' and 'I don't understand', or even 'I don't care'. You have the right to take the time you need to formulate your ideas before expressing them.
- Ask for information or help, i.e. without having negative feelings about your needs.
- Change your mind, to make mistakes and to sometimes act illogically, with full understanding and acceptance of the consequences.
- Like yourself even though you're not perfect, and to sometimes do less than you are capable of doing.
- Have positive, satisfying relationships within which you feel comfortable and free to express yourself honestly, and the right to change or end relationships, if they don't meet your needs.
- Change, enhance or develop your life in any way you determine.

Source: adapted from University of Illinois Counseling Center website
www.couns.uiuc.edu/Brochures/assertiv.htm

ACTIVITY 16

Consider the rights listed above.

Do you agree with them all, or would you delete or change the wording of some of them?

Do you agree with them in theory but find it difficult to implement them in practice?

Do you feel you have additional rights?

You may find it useful to discuss this activity with your colleagues or your team.

FEEDBACK

When you accept the list of rights, or an amended version, for yourself you have to accept that other people also have those rights. The way you communicate will reflect how you view other people as much as how you view yourself.

ACTIVITY 17

Consider the following situations. How could you respond in an assertive manner?

Situation	Assertive response
Your line manager requests that the monthly reports are completed by noon the next day as he's going on holiday and wants to sign them off.	
A new member of your team is late for work and tries to slip in unnoticed.	
Your team is the last to be informed about some important developments which will affect their work routines – by the time you are briefed to tell them, they've heard about it on the grapevine.	

FEEDBACK

Assertive responses involve bringing it to the attention of the other party that the behaviour is unacceptable and agreeing a way forward. In each case it would involve collecting information to substantiate your case, and staying polite and courteous. People tend to respond to assertive behaviour with assertive behaviour. Therefore, if the way in which you communicate is assertive your team is likely to respond in kind.

ACTIVITY 18

Are there any situations in which you might decide it is more appropriate to behave either aggressively or passively?

FEEDBACK

There may be an emergency situation where aggressive behaviour is appropriate. Alternatively, you may recognize that you don't have the confidence to behave assertively or that it would intimidate someone, if they themselves were lacking in confidence. What's important is that you become sensitive to the way in which you communicate and reflect on how you handled specific situations.

Attitudes and assumptions

Our attitudes and the assumptions have a significant impact on how we communicate.

Everyone has their own personal belief and value system formed as a result of:

- the way they live and were brought up (i.e. a person's culture)
- the messages they receive from the media (e.g. television, newspapers)
- knowledge, or lack of it, about a particular topic.

Our beliefs influence our attitudes towards people which in turn influence how we communicate.

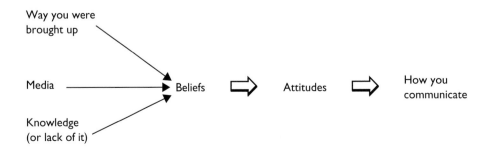

ACTIVITY 19

Typical attitudes of non-disabled people towards people with disabilities include embarrassment, fear of not behaving appropriately, or pity.

Identify two factors in society which have contributed towards people developing these attitudes?

How might these attitudes show in a person's manner of communicating with someone, e.g. in a wheelchair?

FEEDBACK

Attitudes towards people with disabilities are a result of:

- The ways schools used to be organized, segregating disabled and non-disabled children.
- Lack of knowledge.
- Messages in the news media that reinforce images of disabled people as needy, grateful, deserving, plucky or brave. These images underline ideas that disabled people are separate from non-disabled people.
- Charities – in raising money they give prominence to differences and show that people with disabilities need help.

FEEDBACK

The classic response is the 'Does he take sugar attitude?' with people directing questions to anyone but the person in the wheelchair. Feeling patronized or excluded are other common feelings reported by disabled people resulting from society's attitudes.

Attitudes are a common basis for grouping people together based on a characteristic they share and then making assumptions about them. Known as stereotypical assumptions they can be about the way a group of people will behave, about what they want or about their capabilities. For example:

She's Asian ... she'll like to go for a curry.

He's blind ... he won't want to come to the cinema with us.

She's got children ... she won't want to go to the conference in Paris.

Each of the statements contains a stereotypical assumption. They're all based on a group of people together with a particular characteristic, and then an assumption has been made about everyone belonging to that group. Common stereotypical assumptions are related to gender, racial origin, disability, social background, sexual orientation and cultural background.

Stereotypical assumptions, more often than not, simply aren't true. The danger is that common stereotypical assumptions often lead to completely unfounded prejudice (an unfavourable belief about someone) which leads to discrimination (unfair treatment). Again if you are making negative assumptions about someone then, it will underpin and cloud your whole relationship with them.

Stereotypical assumptions are just one example of how attitudes affect behaviour and the way we communicate. We all have values and beliefs which we have absorbed, since childhood and assume that our way is the 'normal' way. It's human nature. However, this can lead to the belief that anyone who does not conform to our values and beliefs:

- should change their ways, or
- should be ashamed of themselves, or
- behaves in an unacceptable way.

If we identify one way of doing things as normal, there is a danger of implying that other ways are 'abnormal'. Once this happens it opens the way for prejudice, and will ultimately affect the way we communicate with someone. It's virtually impossible to hide your true feelings about someone; you may choose your words carefully but what you really believe will seep through your body language and the way you talk.

CHALLENGING NEGATIVE ATTITUDES AND ASSUMPTIONS

Attitudes and assumptions are complex, and often people need to 'unlearn' many beliefs they developed as children in order to, using Harris's terminology, reach an I'm OK – You're OK position. It's not easy. The very nature of a *belief* is that it is right – that it is a fact of life.

The only way that you check your beliefs about what is normal or acceptable is to ask yourself the questions:

- Why do I think that?
- What makes my way better?
- Could I explain to someone else why my way is better?

A narrow view of what is 'normal' or 'right' does not stand up to close scrutiny.

As with negative attitudes, recognizing stereotypical assumptions is also difficult – it means accepting that a belief you hold is not true. To combat discrimination based on stereotypical assumptions people have to get into the habit of asking the question: *What makes me think that?* If your answer is that it is because a person has a characteristic which groups him or her with others (he's deaf, she's black, he's gay, he's Muslim, he's too old) then your attitudes are likely to be unfounded rather than being based on facts.

ACTIVITY 20

Identify an occasion when someone at work communicated that they disapproved of something about you, without actually saying it.

- How did you pick up the message?

- What affect did it have on your relationship with that person?

FEEDBACK

It's almost impossible to prevent communicating the way you view people towards them. As a manager, who needs to communicate positively and build relationships with a wide range of people, it's essential that you review your underlying attitudes and assumptions.

You may find it useful to use the 'ladder of inference' to test your conclusions against the information available. The ladder shows the process which happens in our minds between receiving data and taking actions based on the data. There are seven rungs to the ladder, as shown in Figure 2.1.

The ladder shows how we select out data from our observations and experiences, and add meaning to them based on our existing beliefs to form the basis of how we behave. In other words, our actions are based on our interpretation of information – not necessarily on reality.

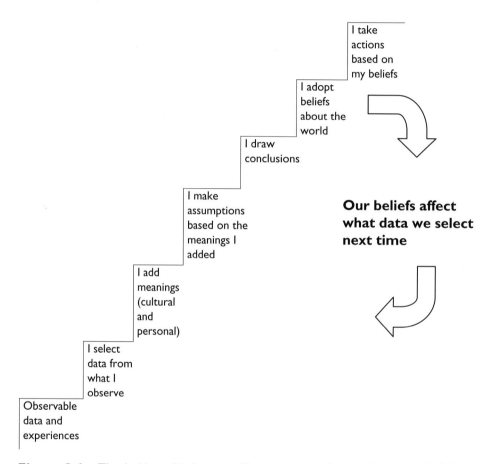

Figure 2.1   The ladder of inference. (*Source*: adapted from Senge *et al.* (1994) *The Fifth Discipline Fieldbook*, Nicholas Brearley Publishing, 24.)

ACTIVITY 21

Identify an occasion when you jumped to a conclusion that turned out to be wrong. Use the ladder below to identify what made you come to the conclusion. You may not stick strictly to all the steps outlined above; what's important is the thought you put into unpicking and understanding the mental processes which determine how you interact with people.

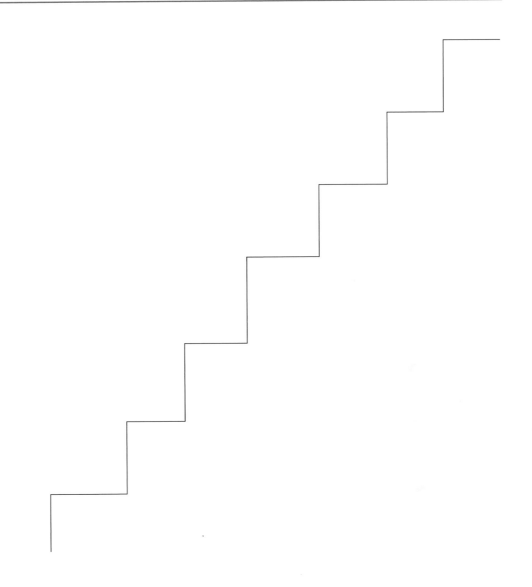

FEEDBACK

Being aware of the process of jumping to conclusions can help you to check your own, often inaccurate, conclusions before you use them as a basis for behaviour:

We live in a world of self-generating beliefs which remain largely untested. We adopt those beliefs because they are based on conclusions, which are inferred from what we observe, plus our past experiences. Our ability to achieve the results we truly desire is eroded by our feelings that:

- *our beliefs are the truth*
- *the truth is obvious*
- *our beliefs are based on real data*
- *the data we select are the real data.*

Ross[2]

Trust

Trust is the knowledge that you will not deliberately or accidentally, consciously or unconsciously take advantage of me.

Douglas McGregor

The ways in which messages are received are often very dependent on the level of trust between the two parties.

ACTIVITY 22

What's the difference between trusting and trustworthy behaviour?

FEEDBACK

Trustworthy behaviour includes being honest, keeping promises and always acting ethically. An important trait of any manager is to be trustworthy so that your team and colleagues feel confident in discussing their ideas and opinions openly. You have to use your judgement to select who to trust depending on their past record.

> People who have the trustworthiness competence[3]:
>
> - Act ethically and are above reproach
> - Build trust through their reliability and authenticity
> - Admit their mistakes and confront unethical actions in others
> - Take tough, principled stands even if they are unpopular.
>
> Goleman[3]

In his book *The Seven Habits of Highly Effective People*, Covey[4] illustrates the connection between trust and co-operation and resulting levels of communication.

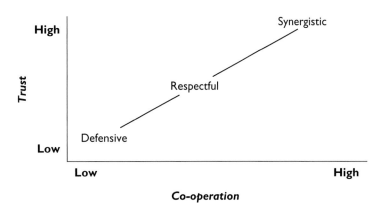

Source: adapted from Covey, S. (1989)[4]

When trust and co-operation are low, communication becomes defensive. As trust and co-operation increase you get 'respectful communication'. This is polite communication where people interact but fail to remove barriers and open up. Finally, where trust and co-operation are high both parties are able to be open, honest and creative. This creates synergy which results in both parties benefiting from the exchange.

ACTIVITY 23

The following activity asks you to consider aspects of openness and trust in your team. You may find it useful to consider members of your team individually as you consider the second group of questions.

1 Do you:	Yes	No
Discuss how to make improvements with your team?	❏	❏
Talk to your team about how you see the work they do?	❏	❏
Share concerns and issues with your team?	❏	❏
Always show trustworthy behaviour?	❏	❏
2 Do members of your team:		
Make suggestions for improvements to you?	❏	❏
Talk to you about how they see the work they do?	❏	❏
Share concerns and issues they have with you?	❏	❏
Trust you?	❏	❏

Trust and openness are pre-requisites of effective team communication. You may need to review your behaviour to ensure:

- you build up a reputation for being trustworthy
- you show that you trust your team members.

TRUST AT AN ORGANIZATIONAL LEVEL

Most managers would see the value of open and honest communication. But the culture of an organization has a huge impact on whether that is a reality.

Organizational culture is a major influence on:

- how organizations communicate
- what they communicate
- the effect of the communication.

Many organizations may have clear channels of communication but the culture of the organization doesn't mean the communication channels will be used or be effective.

So what is culture?

Culture is 'how things are done around here'. It is what is typical of the organisation, the habits, the prevailing attitudes, the grown-up pattern of expected behaviour

Drennan[5]

Often you only need to come into contact with how an organization operates for a short period of time to pick up a sense of what's accepted as the way things are done. You then often unconsciously pick up these methods as you don't realize that you are actually absorbing what you see happening around you.

Different parts of organizations develop different cultures. For example, the culture within an organization's finance team may be very different from its publishing department. However, overriding departments, there's likely to be a dominant culture within an organization with which everyone has to interact.

If an organization's culture is seen as being trustworthy then employees will generally trust internal communications. They know there are no 'hidden agendas' or that truth isn't being held back. Therefore, they will be more likely to respond openly to communications. Conversely in organizations where there is a culture of mistrust and hidden agendas, people will naturally respond cautiously, trying to find the true meaning of what's really going on.

Everyone at work has a choice – whether or not to keep their ideas and opinions to themselves and remain silent, or whether to voice them. Often team members won't feel comfortable raising issues with their line manager for a variety of reasons. Research by Milliken *et al.*[6] has shown that the most frequently mentioned reason for remaining silent was the fear of being viewed or being labelled negatively, followed by a belief that speaking up would make no difference. The outcomes of being viewed negatively are shown in Figure 2.2 with all factors being inter-related and culminating in a negative effect on the person's career opportunities.

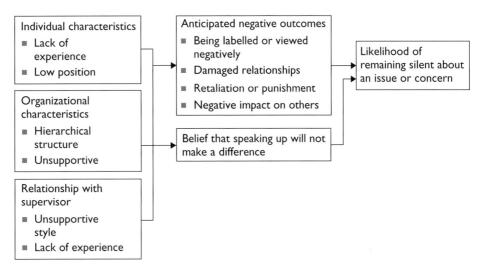

Figure 2.2 A model of the choice to remain silent. (Reproduced with permission from Milliken, F., Morrison, E. and Hewlin, P. (2003) An exploratory study of employee silence: issues that employees don't communicate upwards and why, *Journal of Management Studies*, 40(6), 1467.)

ACTIVITY 24

What do you see as being the implications for an organization with a culture of remaining silent?

A culture of silence will give all levels of management a distorted picture of what's happening in the organization – good news will be reported; issues will be kept hidden. It will also lead to dissatisfaction and frustration amongst employees. In short, it's not a healthy environment for an organization.

Becoming a more effective communicator

Section 1 showed the process of communication to be relatively straight-forward. All you need to do is:

- know what you want to communicate
- consider the needs of who you're communicating with
- choose an appropriate method or 'channel'
- identify how you will get feedback.

However, as this section has shown, there are many factors which influence communication. The more sensitive you are to these, the more effective at communicating you will become.

In their book *Shut Up and Listen!*[7] Theobald and Cooper put forward the following six simple strategies for improving the way you communicate. You may find it useful as a checklist to refer to.

1   **Think about your audience**   This is about putting yourself in the shoes of your audience and being sensitive to how they will receive the messages you send.

2   **Convey conviction**   A message backed up with conviction and passion is infinitely stronger than a half-hearted message. Conviction is not something you can unleash when required. You need to check that you really are convinced before you start.

3   **'Shut up and listen'**   Probably the hardest strategy to practise. Listening gives you thinking time, as well as being courteous and avoiding instances when you speak without having all the facts to hand.

4   **Stay conscious – think and plan**   The more you engage your brain thinking about and planning how to communicate the more effective you'll be. Planning communication isn't a one-off activity; ideally it becomes a state of mind.

5   **Recognize the importance of storytelling**   Try using 'stories' to get over key points or messages. A story can embed a message and help people to understand its context far more effectively than a list of bullet points in a powerpoint presentation.

6 **Be yourself** This final strategy results from having developed an increased awareness of what's involved in communication. Once you re-awakened often dormant skills of effective communication you can afford to relax and enjoy the benefits.

You can also work generally to increase the quality of conversations within your team. Research[8] has shown four main types of conversations taking place in organizations, as shown in Figure 2.3.

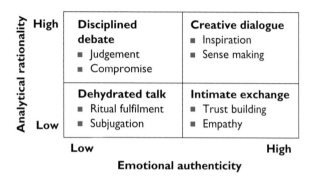

Figure 2.3 Four main types of conversations found within an organization. (*Source:* Gratton and Ghoshal[8])

When listening to conversations in companies all over the world, it was found that most of the conversations witnessed over 5 years were **dehydrated** with participants going through the motions of communications rather than actively engaging. The goal for any organization would be to have more:

■ **Disciplined debate** Conversations focused on intellectual questioning and rational arguments.

■ **Intimate exchange** These conversations re-personalize the workplace and recognize that employees have feelings and emotions. Conversations about feelings.

■ **Creative dialogue** Deep rich conversations.

To improve the quality of conversations they suggest you can:

■ Create a trusting environment in which people feel confident to question and doubt.

■ Create time and space for conversations.

■ Legitimize people to ask big broad questions.

■ Encourage diversity – observations suggest conversations amongst dissimilar people are often more stimulating than conversations among similar people (in an atmosphere of trust and mutual respect).

ACTIVITY 25

First focus on your organization as a whole and assess to what extent you think:

	100%	Not at all

- There is an environment of trust within your organization generally?

- Sufficient time and space is given to conversations

- People feel confident to raise big broad questions?

- Diversity is encouraged?

Now consider your team. To what extent do you think:

	100%	Not at all

- There is an environment of trust?

- Sufficient time and space is given to conversations

- Team members feel confident to raise big broad questions?

- Diversity is encouraged?

FEEDBACK

The way you communicate and the culture of communication in your team is dependent on you. It's an area where you have control and can improve. The importance of developing your inter-personal skills can't be overstated. This section has given only a taste of the many theories that attempt to explain how we behave. In practice the theories are interesting but it is allocating thinking time to reflecting on what's really going on around you that will make the difference to your competence as a manager.

ACTIVITY 26

Identify an important message that you will have to communicate verbally but which is not simply information. For example, it may be a message to a team member who is underperforming, or excelling.

- What is the message you want to convey?

- When and how will you communicate?

- What aspects of your body language will contribute towards conveying the message?

- Are there any specific words you want to use?

- How will you ensure that you convey your message assertively?

- Do you need to explore any attitudes or assumptions which may be inaccurate?

- How do you think the person may respond?

■ How will you make sure that your message has been received?

■ How will you ensure that the conversation contributes to having a good long-term relationship with this person?

FEEDBACK

It would be impossible, and unnecessary, to think through everything you want to communicate in this way. However, by planning a few important communications, you will find that the skills you use will automatically transfer into routine use.

Learning summary

- What you are like as a person influences how you communicate and interpret messages?
- Your effectiveness as a manager is likely to increase the more you:
  - recognize that there are many factors which affect the communication process
  - become sensitive to the way it affects how you communicate.
- Your state of mind will affect how you communicate. Berne[9] identified the following three main states: adult, parent and child. Adult–adult transactions are the most productive in the working environment.
- Behaviour can be categorized as being assertive, aggressive or passive. Assertive behaviour is about having the confidence to express your needs, feelings and opinions openly, and respect other people when they express theirs.
- Attitudes and assumptions make a significant impact on how we communicate. Try to get into the habit of challenging any negative attitudes and assumptions you may have.
- The ways in which messages are received are often very dependent on the level of trust between the two parties.
- A manager must be trustworthy at all times to gain the confidence of team members. You have to use your judgement to select who you can trust.

- To become a more effective communicator:
  - think about your audience
  - convey conviction
  - shut up and listen
  - stay conscious – think and plan
  - recognize the importance of story telling
  - be yourself.
- To improve the quality of conversations:
  - create a trusting environment in which people feel confident to question and doubt
  - create time and space for conversations
  - legitimize people to ask big broad questions
  - encourage diversity – observations suggest conversations amongst dissimilar people are often more stimulating than conversations among similar people (in an atmosphere of trust and mutual respect).

Into the workplace

You need to:

- Communicate using an adult state of mind
- Recognize assertive behaviour
- Challenge your attitudes and assumptions
- Increase the level of trust within your team.

References

1   Berne, E. (1961) *Transactional Analysis in Psychotherapy*, Grove Press, New York

2   Ross, R. in Senge *et al.* (1994) *The Fifth Discipline Fieldbook*, Nicholas Brearley, p. 242

3   Goleman, D. (1998) *Working with Emotional Intelligence*, Bloomsbury

4   Covey, S. (1989) *The Seven Habits of Highly Effective People*, Simon & Schuster, p. 270

5   Drennan, D. (1992) *Transforming Company Culture*, McGraw-Hill

6   Milliken, F., Morrison, E. and Hewlin, P. (2003) An exploratory study of employee silence: issues that employees don't communicate upwards and why. *Journal of Management Studies* 40(6), 1453–1476

7   Theobald, T. and Cooper, C. (2004) *Shut Up and Listen*! Kogan Page

8   Gratton, L. and Ghoshal, S. (2002) *Organisational Dynamics*, 31(3), 209–223

9   Berne, E. (1964) *Games People Play*, Penguin

Section 3 Communicating at work

Introduction

To handle yourself, use your head; to handle others, use your heart.

Donald Laird

The first two sections looked at the process of communication and some of the factors which affect the context in which messages are sent and received. They gave the framework for what happens whenever we interact with other people.

This section looks at a variety of work situations which involve tailoring the communication process to meet specific objectives. It covers the skills involved in:

- giving feedback
- influencing
- networking
- negotiating
- making a presentation.

Giving feedback

Giving feedback on performance is an essential skill for any manager.

ACTIVITY 27

When do you give feedback to team members?

FEEDBACK

Most organizations have some form of performance appraisal system in which each appraisal meeting involves the three main stages of:

1   reviewing performance against existing work objectives (including giving feedback)

↓

2   setting new/revised work objectives

↓

3   identifying and planning to meet development needs.

In addition, line managers may also take on responsibility for directly developing team members, e.g. by delegating, coaching, which also involve the process of giving feedback.

However, giving feedback to your team should be an integral part of daily routine. It doesn't have to be formal; a few words of appreciation or encouragement can have a positive impact on motivation. Motivation is the inner drive that makes us do things. One theory about motivation was put forward by Maslow.[1] He identified that people have the following needs:

■   The need to maintain our bodies, i.e. with food and water.
■   The need to feel safe from danger.
■   Social needs, which include the need to feel we belong and are liked (e.g. by colleagues) and loved (e.g. by family).
■   The need to feel good about your yourself.
■   The need to feel personal satisfaction from achievements.

Maslow saw the different needs as a hierarchy and that people would be motivated to meet their various needs, starting at the bottom of the hierarchy. As needs at the bottom of the hierarchy are met, people can then focus on meeting higher needs (Figure 3.1).

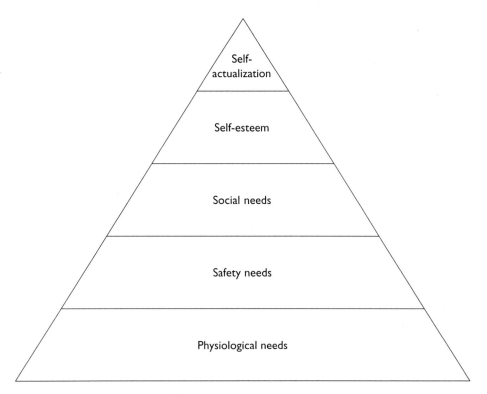

Figure 3.1   Maslow's hierarchy of needs

Which 'need' can 'receiving constructive feedback' on your performance contribute towards?

FEEDBACK

Receiving constructive feedback can contribute to increased levels of self-esteem, which in turn can contribute towards increased motivation to work.

| Communicating that you value a person by giving feedback on their work | → | Fulfilling a person's self-esteem needs, i.e. makes them feel good | → | Feeling motivated to work to receive further feedback |

ACTIVITY 29

What is the likely effect of failing to give feedback on your team members' performance or giving feedback in a destructive manner?

FEEDBACK

Failing to give feedback is likely to demotivate members of your team and lead to a decline in performance.

HOW TO GIVE FEEDBACK THAT MOTIVATES

When you give feedback make sure you do the following:

- Find a place i.e. private, to give the feedback.
- Start with highlighting positive aspects, i.e. the good news.
- Focus on the behaviour, not a person's personality. For example, 'that customer seemed quite confused with the directions you gave her', rather than 'you're useless at communicating with people'.
- Give the feedback soon after the event.
- Have enough time – feedback shouldn't be rushed.
- Ask for your team member's point of view, and *listen* to their response.
- Agree or suggest actions which they could take to improve – record what you agree.
- End on an encouraging, positive note.

ACTIVITY 30

Identify an occasion when you gave feedback to a team member. Do you think the way in which you communicated the feedback helped to motivate him or her?

FEEDBACK

Try to get into the habit of asking your team if they find your feedback useful and how it can be improved. The degree to which team members will engage and give you feedback can be a measure of your success at having created an environment in which they feel they can be open and honest.

Influencing

An effective manager needs to be good at influencing people to be able to modify either attitudes or behaviours. Influencing involves being skilled at communicating.

> **People who have this competence:**
>
> ■ are skilled at winning people over
> ■ fine-tune presentations to appeal to the listener
> ■ use complex strategies like indirect influence to build consensus and support
> ■ orchestrate dramatic events to effectively make a point.[2]

Critical to influencing people is being able to understanding their point of view; in other words 'where they are coming from'.

ACTIVITY 31

What key skills of communicating do you have to employ to understand someone else's viewpoint?

FEEDBACK

Being responsive to a person's non-verbal behaviour as well as listening attentively are both necessary if you are going to empathize with another person's view. Also important is building rapport and taking time to build bonds based on something you have in common.

> In a study of strategic decisions at 356 American companies, more than half were never adopted, were implemented only partially, or were abandoned at the outset. The most common reason for the failure of these plans was that the lead executives were imperious, trying to impose their ideas instead of building supporting consensus. Where the imperious approach was employed, 58 per cent of the time the result was failure. But when executives first conferred with colleagues to rethink their long-term priorities, strategic plans were adopted 96 per cent of the time. As Paul McNutt, the Ohio State University Professor of Management who did the study says, 'If you involve people in some of the steps of the process, they will become missionaries for you'.[2]

Handy, in *Understanding Organizations*,[3] identified five main sources of power which can be exerted when influencing people:

Sources of power	Methods of influence based on one or more sources of power
■ **Physical power** This is power associated with an overwhelming physical presence that can be real or perceived (e.g. in the case of bullies).	**Force** This is influencing through the use or threat of physical power.
■ **Resource power** This is power which stems from having resources to reward (e.g. promotion, overtime, time-off).	**Rules and procedures** This involves setting up rules and procedures so that people comply. Needs both resource and position power.
■ **Position power** This is the power which comes from holding a particular degree of authority within an organization. You have position power over your team; your line manager has position power over you.	**Exchange** This involves influencing behaviour through the exchange of resources (e.g. negotiating, bribing). Again this requires resource and position power.
■ **Expert power** This is the power that comes from being an acknowledged expert on a topic.	**Persuasion** In its purist form this method of influencing relies on the power of argument and logic. Can rely on a combination of expert and personal power.

- **Personal power**   This can be referred to a charisma. The source of power stems from the personality of the person rather than external influences

Ecology   Handy uses the term ecology to describe how changing work practices and the work environment can influence behaviour, e.g. setting up a divisional structure in a relatively small organization was bound to fuel an empire-building attitude; dismantle the divisional structure and the organization united. Usually requires a combination of resource, position and personal power.

Magnetism   This involves influencing through interpersonal relationships based on trust, using charm, respect or attraction and is based on personal power.

ACTIVITY 33

What practical lessons can you apply from a combination of Goleman's and Handy's perspectives on influencing?

FEEDBACK

You are likely to use all of the sources of power for influencing people, apart from physical power, at different times. What's important is to:

- recognize the power source you are using
- use effective communication skills with whichever method you are using – don't think that a particular power source negates the necessity of communicating effectively.

ACTIVITY 33

Identify an occasion when you recently had to influence the attitude or behaviour of someone at work.

- What power source(s) did you use?

■ Did you take steps to understand the other person's starting point?

■ Did you tune into their non-verbal behaviour?

■ Did you listen to what they said?

FEEDBACK

Increasing your influencing skills involves becoming conscious of the impact your behaviour has on other people. Once again, there is no alternative to spending some time reflecting on what has happened, or observing other people who are successful at influencing, to develop your skills.

Networking

Networks are at the heart of most organizations and involve managers building up contacts outside the normal line management structure so informal conversations can help either or both parties. It leads to an informal reservoir of ideas, information, advice and support that you can tap into.

Networking is about using opportunities around you so that:

■ you can help others
■ others can help you.

It involves building relationships based on mutual support and trust. The emphasis has to be in the word *mutual*. Focusing solely on people you perceive as potentially being useful to you isn't networking.

An effective networker concentrates on being helpful to other people. By proactively building trust and respect you will then find that most people will respond in kind. Being successful at networking involves getting right the delicate balance between dedicating too much time or too little time to networking. Time spent on networking often doesn't seem to contribute directly to work objectives; therefore, it's often easier to ignore the potential to build relationships with people around you.

Your ability to network relies heavily on your communicating skills. You need to be:

- wary of assumptions clouding your view of people
- genuinely interested in other people
- listening to people
- remembering what they say (a result of being genuinely interested and listening)
- asking questions
- behaving assertively
- 100 per cent trustworthy – all of the time.

Aim to build your network with people both inside your organization and outside. For example, you may include colleagues, managers in other operational functions, people with specific expertise, suppliers, customers, friends, family members and contacts of family members. Don't worry if you cannot immediately identify a way of helping someone else. By building a relationship, the potential for networking then exists.

ACTIVITY 34

Consider your current network. Make a note of the names of people with whom you have built a relationship and have the potential for networking:

- connected with your current organization

- connected with previous organizations you have worked for

- friends

- family connections

- others

FEEDBACK

Aim to build up your network over time. The first step is building a relationship and that's dependent on investing a little time and energy as well as communicating effectively.

Negotiating

Negotiation is about reaching an agreement which is often a compromise. Two parties have different objectives, each party has to accept a different outcome to accommodate the other party's position.

Negotiation is the skill of trading off differences to reach a win–win agreement for both parties.

O'Connor and Prior[4]

Traditionally, the term *negotiation* has been connected with formal situations which both parties recognize and prepare to try to get the best deal for themselves, e.g. negotiating a pay deal, negotiating a contract, etc. However, if you look upon negotiation as part of the give and take of normal relationships then the skills of negotiation can be applied in a much wider context.

ACTIVITY 35

Consider each of the following models of leadership outlined below. For each one briefly identify where the skills of negotiation are appropriate.

Model 1

The leadership model developed by Tannenbaum and Schmidt[5] is a continuum with **autocratic** at one end and **democratic** at the other. It focuses on how decisions are made within a team. The style of leadership adopted by a manager will depend on the manager's own personality and experiences, the characteristics of team members and the context in which the work takes place (nature of work, culture of the organization, etc.).

Autocratic					Democratic
Manager takes decision alone, without any consultation	Manager takes decision alone but 'sells' benefits to team members	Manager presents ideas for discussion and **pretends** to consult (already has chosen preferred option)	Manager presents ideas for discussion and genuinely consults	Manager presents ideas and asks team to decide – subject to certain limits and boundaries	Manager joins the team in decision-making process

In which styles of leadership would the skills of negotiation be most relevant in the Tannenbaum–Schmidt model?

Model 2

Professor McGregor[6] states that there are two main types of managers: 'Theory X' and 'Theory Y'. Theory X managers have little regard for people, tend to be very authoritarian and, generally, are highly unlikely to be able to motivate anyone to work willingly. Theory Y managers take a quite different view – believing that people are capable of undertaking responsible and creative work and accepting that people will work willingly and well providing that they understand and are committed to whatever it is they are doing.

Which type of manager would be most likely to use negotiation skills?

Model 3

Hersey and Blanchard[7] theory of situational leadership advocates that effective managers adapt their style to suit the situation. They identified four main styles of leadership:

- **Directing style**   A manager using a directing style will be decisive and give instructions as to how things should be done. They expect people to follow orders, carry out tasks in accordance with their requirements and see things their way. They may find it difficult to let go and let people get on with things in their own way.
- **Coaching style**   Using this style the manager is good at involving people in the decision-making process and is willing to take the time and trouble to help people solve problems. They may become too involved with discussions about people's problems which have to be made.
- **Supporting style**   This style allows people to take responsibility but know that the manager is there to give support when needed. The manager is willing to listen and offer wholehearted support.
- **Delegating style**   Managers are good at giving people the freedom to develop their own ideas and take ownership of major tasks and projects. They are willing to let go and trust team members to do a good job on their own.

In which styles of leadership would the skills of negotiation be most relevant in the Hersey–Blanchard model?

FEEDBACK

Negotiation skills are most relevant when a manager engages with team members and they work together to achieve the team's objectives. Negotiation is a part of normal human interaction and, according to the theorists, the following types of managers will find negotiation skills used regularly in daily operations:

- Managers who tend towards a democratic style
- Theory Y managers
- Managers who coach, support and delegate.

COMMUNICATION SKILLS AND NEGOTIATING

Negotiations have three main steps:

Step 1 both sides outline their preferred option

Step 2 a series of offers/suggestions/new ideas as both sides discuss and modify their preferred option

Step 3 both sides reach an agreement.

ACTIVITY 36

Do you mainly agree or disagree with the following statement?
The closer the agreement is to your preferred option, the more successful you have been in the negotiation:

- ❏ Agree
- ❏ Neither agree not disagree
- ❏ Disagree

FEEDBACK

The measure of success of a negotiation is the degree to which both parties are satisfied with the agreement reached, particularly in an on-going relationship. As you discuss each other's preferred options, you may identify another option, or your understanding or view may change. Therefore, to consider an agreement which does not match your preferred option as being a failure will prevent you from being flexible and creative within the discussion.

The following eight behaviours for successful negotiation were identified by Honey in his book *Improve Your People Skills*[8]:

- **Focus on interests not positions**   This is about concentrating on *what* you want to achieve and not necessarily the means of achieving what you identified. For example, you may think that the only way of meeting a deadline would be to take on temporary staff; an alternative may be delaying another project so that a member of staff could work on the priority project.
- **Explore proposals rather than put counter proposals**   This involves listening before speaking.
- **Ask questions**   This is an essential part of exploring the other person's proposal; it also enables you to gather information which can be used as a basis for identifying new options.
- **Summarize**   You need to be able to keep track of a discussion and make sure both you and the other person are clear and in agreement about the outcome.
- **Stick to facts rather than exaggerating**   Otherwise the emotional temperature can become destructive.
- **Attack the problem, not the person**   As with any feedback, comments should be related to the other person's proposal and not degenerate into general comments about the person's competence.
- **Disagree constructively**   This involves giving reasons for disagreeing, not just stating that you disagree and moving on.
- **Be open**   Trust is the key in any relationship. If people know they can trust you they can focus on the negotiation rather than protecting themselves.

ACTIVITY 37

Identify an occasion at work which involved negotiating. Assess yourself against Honey's eight behaviours.

Did I	Yes I did this effectively	Room to improve	No and it wasn't relevant
Focus on interests not positions	☐	☐	☐
Explore proposals rather than putting counter proposals	☐	☐	☐
Ask questions	☐	☐	☐
Summarize	☐	☐	☐
Stick to facts rather than exaggerating	☐	☐	
Attack the problem, not the person	☐	☐	☐
Disagree constructively	☐	☐	☐
Focus on being open	☐	☐	☐

FEEDBACK

Being alert to the interpersonal skills involved in effective negotiation is an important step in integrating them into your daily encounters. Often difficulties arise in identifying that a discussion is a negotiation, and therefore opportunities to use Honey's eight behaviours in practice are missed.

Delivering a presentation or briefing

Delivering a presentation or briefing is often equated with 'delivering information'. Instead of sending out documents, a person stands up in front of a group and tells them what's happening. It equates a briefing with a one-way communication process, made more palatable because there is a human face delivering the information rather than in the written form.

Delivering an effective presentation depends on good communication skills to engage the audience. It has to become a two-way process.

You need to do the following.

KNOW WHAT YOU WANT TO ACHIEVE

A briefing can be an opportunity to achieve one or more of the following:

- gather feedback
- gauge opinion
- exchange ideas
- motivate
- influence
- get buy-in.

You need to be clear about your purpose before you start to plan how to deliver the briefing.

In a survey of 669 organizations, 75 per cent think that feedback from team briefings is the most effective listening method.

Industrial Society[9]

KNOW YOUR AUDIENCE

Knowing your audience is important. Otherwise your presentation is based on assumptions which can become a recipe for disaster. If you are briefing your team then you'll know their background and what they bring to the briefing. If not, then take the time to find out, e.g.

- What is their prior knowledge?
- What do they want to get out of the briefing, if anything?
- What attitudes might be present in the group?
- Are there any specific needs related to hearing, sight or mobility that you need to take into consideration?

It's about putting yourself in the shoes of your audience *before* you plan how to deliver the briefing.

MAKE IT TWO WAY

There are a number of techniques that you can use in briefing sessions to make sure you interact with your audience and it becomes two way, e.g.

- **Ask questions**   Questions can range from simple ones requiring a short answer designed mainly to establish communication to questions, that initiate detailed discussions and explore feelings and attitudes. Don't fall into the trap of asking questions for the sake of it. The audience will soon feel patronized and rapport will be difficult to establish. Questions must have a purpose, e.g. to check knowledge, obtain information, stimulate thought, gather feedback. Sometimes it may be helpful to pose a rhetorical question to focus the audience's mind on an aspect. Typically these are used at the start of a presentation when you pose a rhetorical question that your presentation will then answer. Alternatively, they can be used at the end of a presentation to give 'food for thought' and stimulate further thought.

Types of questions

Questions can be:

- **Closed**   only require a one or two word answer, often either yes or no
- **Open**   requiring a fuller answer.

Most open questions begin with one of the following words:

- **What**   'What do you think of …?'
- **How**   'How do you know that will happen?'
- **Why**   'Why does he respond like that?'
- **Where**   'Where do you see the problem lying?'
- **When**   'When is that most likely to occur?'

ACTIVITY 38

What might be a danger of asking too many open questions during a presentation?

FEEDBACK

It's difficult to manage the response to open questions if the audience is large (over 15 people). Answers to open questions may also widen discussion to areas which you don't want to explore. Therefore, take care when asking questions. You have to be able to deal with the response.

- **Introduce group activities**   These can be used to fully engage the audience and encourage their contribution; dividing the audience into groups and allocating a task to each group to feedback to the main audience, involves everyone and builds on their inputs. Often this is far more enjoyable for the audience than simply listening to what someone else has to say.
- **Hold a discussion**   Again, this gives the opportunity for everyone to be involved. We look at how to manage a discussion in the next section on meetings.

ACTIVITY 39

What implications has the size of your audience got on the extent to which you can make a presentation two way?

FEEDBACK

The larger the audience, the less opportunities you have for making it two way. It is more difficult to engage with a large audience. Instead of encouraging dialogue within the presentation you have to rely on your use of body language and tone of voice as well as clarity of your message.

PLAN THE DETAIL

The type of briefing you deliver can vary from being almost totally scripted by someone else in the organization to one that you prepare yourself to meet your own specific objectives. In the latter case, you will have to devote time and thought to preparing the content. If you are given a briefing to deliver you need to familiarize yourself with the content and make sure you still go through the three steps described above.

Preparation involves knowing:

- what you are going to say
- how you are going to say it
- how and when you are going to make the communication two way
- what visual aids and handouts you want to use (and prepare them beforehand).

Always make sure you have notes to guide you through the delivery, for example:

Team briefing July 1

1   Welcome, 30 minutes to consider: What are we going to do next?

2   **Input** results of customer survey

Use slides 1–5

3   **Ask**: the reactions to survey results (flipchart responses)

4   **Input** implications for organization

Use slides 6–9

5   **Divide** into functional groups: What does it mean for us? (allow 5–10 minutes)

Your notes should act as a prompt to follow a planned structure. Don't try to put too much detail into the notes – you should know the content.

RELAX AND DELIVER

Many people are nervous at the prospect of standing up in front of a group of people. Some degree of nervousness is good and serves a useful purpose. Having increased levels of adrenaline can sharpen your performance. However, too much nervousness, or lack of confidence, can block your ability to use your body language to engage the audience.

ACTIVITY 40

What are the signs of someone who is lacking in confidence when delivering a briefing?

FEEDBACK

They will often be reluctant to use eye contact and talk too fast so that the meaning is lost. They become too focused on the situation rather than achieving the purpose of the presentation. It's very difficult for the audience to engage and develop a rapport with the person presenting (just as it's difficult to hold a conversation with someone whose mind is miles away). If you are prone to nervousness then:

- make sure you prepare thoroughly – the knowledge that you've prepared well gives confidence
- don't talk unless you have eye contact – force yourself if you have to
- always talk to the audience – never to a slide or flipchart
- have a glass of water handy just in case your mouth goes dry
- take deep breaths
- remember that the audience wants to be engaged and interested – that's what matters to them.

We had snakes in Raiders of the Lost Ark and bugs in Indiana Jones and The Temple of Doom. But supposedly, man's greatest fear is public speaking. That'll be in our next picture.

Steven Spielberg (whose greatest fear is public speaking)

ACTIVITY 41

Identify a briefing you will deliver. Consider the following points:

- What is the purpose of the briefing?
  - ❐ give information
  - ❐ gather feedback
  - ❐ gauge opinion
  - ❐ exchange ideas
  - ❐ motivate
  - ❐ influence
  - ❐ get buy-in.

- What do you know about your audience?

- What techniques will you use to make the presentation two way?

FEEDBACK

Always put yourself in the shoes of the audience when you are planning a briefing – if you would find it interesting and riveting so will they; if you see it as an exercise in delivering information, a one-way communication exercise will result in reducing its impact and lose its value.

Learning summary

- The way you communicate directly affects your effectiveness as a manager.
- You need to tailor the way you communicate depending on the situation.
- The way you communicate feedback directly affects the motivation levels of your team members. Regularly review your behaviour against the feedback checklist given earlier in the section and ask for feedback from your team members.
- Being able to influence people relies on using a variety of sources of power. Communication skills which are particularly important include:
  - being responsive to their non-verbal behaviour
  - listening attentively
  - empathizing with the other person's viewpoint
  - building a rapport.
- Networking involves building up contacts outside the normal line management structure. It involves building relationships based on mutual support, respect and trust.
- Negotiating is about reaching an agreement which is often a compromise. It's part of normal interaction within the workplace and is used more often by managers with a more democratic and participative style of management.
- Delivering a presentation of briefing depends on good communication to engage the audience. You need to:
  - know what you want to achieve
  - know your audience
  - make it two way (e.g. by asking questions, introducing group activities, holding a discussion)
  - plan the detail.

Into the workplace

You need to:

- plan and reflect on the way you communicate whenever you interact with people.

References

1   Maslow, A. (1998) *Toward a Psychology of Being*, 3rd edn. Wiley, New York

2   Goleman, D. (1998) *Working With Emotional Intelligence*, Bloomsbury

3   Handy, C. (1993) *Understanding Organizations*, Penguin

4   O'Connor, J. and Prior, R. (1995) *Successful Selling with NLP*, Thorsons

5   Tannenbaum, R. and Schmidt, W. (1973) *How to Choose a Leadership Pattern*, Harvard Business Review

6   McGregor, D. (1985) *Human Side of Enterprise*, McGraw-Hill Education

7   Hersey, P. and Blanchard, K. (1982) *Management of Organizational Behaviour*, Prentice Hall

8   Honey, P. (1988) *Improve Your People Skills*, Chartered Institute of Personnel and Development

9   The Industrial Society, *Team Communications*, *Managing Best Practice*, June 2000

Section 4 Making meetings work

Introduction

James Houghton, then the CEO of Cornering made a rule that anyone who believed that he or she added no value in a particular meeting of regular frequency, nor obtained any value, could take his or her name off the list of participants for that meeting. A very large number of ritualized meetings died very quickly.

Gratton and Ghoshal[1]

In many organizations meetings are seen as huge time wasters and an excuse for procrastination and indecisiveness. As illustrated by the quote above, many people attend meetings who simply have no need to be there. The action of calling a meeting can give a feel-good factor; something has happened and any related work or decisions can justifiably be postponed until the meeting. Sometimes an 'if in doubt, call a meeting' syndrome pervades an organization – as long as progress is seen to be being made it doesn't matter how slow and tortuous that progress might be.

As a manager you are likely to call and chair team meetings as well as attend a variety of different types of meetings across your organization. In this section of the workbook we explore the skills and considerations for both chairing and contributing to meetings.

Types of meetings

The term 'meeting' is a catch-all term to describe anything from a brief exchange of ideas or information in a corridor to a very formal, regulated meeting of, for example, shareholders or directors.

ACTIVITY 42

Make a list of meetings you have attended in the last month.

Improptu meetings, e.g. by chance in a corridor	Planned work-related meetings	Formal meetings

Estimate, roughly, the amount of time you spend in meetings in an average week. Include time spent travelling.

FEEDBACK

Planned work-related meetings are likely to take up a substantial amount of your time; some managers spend more than 60 per cent of their time in meetings. It's important that this time is used effectively and kept to a minimum.

Who's who in a meeting

Meetings need someone to take control and lead them. This is the role of the 'chair' and involves the following:

■ **Preparing for the meeting**   Making sure the necessary people are invited, putting together an agenda, distributing any papers (this work may be delegated to a secretary).

■ **Running the meeting**   The chair is in charge of the meeting and is responsible for opening the meeting, ensuring the agenda is followed, making sure everyone has an opportunity to contribute, summarizing points raised and actions agreed.

All formal meetings, and those with more than five or six participants, will need a 'chair'. Sometimes, for example in a committee, the role of chair is a permanent position. In workplace meetings the chair can be appointed to run a specific meeting. As manager you are likely to chair your team meetings. However, encouraging other people to take on the role can be an excellent development opportunity as well as giving you an opportunity to focus on participating in the meeting.

Meetings also need someone to take the minutes, i.e. make a written record of what happened during the meeting. In formal situations this is the role of the 'secretary'. However, in less formal meetings it can be any participant who is willing to take on the role.

Reasons for holding meetings

Meetings have to have a least one purpose.

ACTIVITY 43

Consider three different meetings you have attended recently. Identify the purpose(s) of each meeting by ticking the appropriate column. There is space for you to add additional purposes of the meeting.

	Meeting 1	Meeting 2	Meeting 3
Information giving/updating			
Reviewing progress			
Decision-making			
Problem-solving			
Planning			
Consultation			
Team-building			
Other			

FEEDBACK

It's likely that the meetings you attend have a variety of purposes. For example, an appraisal meeting will be about reviewing progress and planning. A team meeting may combine updating, problem-solving and planning activities.

Before any meeting you should be able to answer the questions:

- Why is this meeting being held?
- What should be achieved as a result of this meeting?

If you are unclear, or you found the question difficult to answer, then you need to take action by either getting clarification or re-considering the need for the meeting. Even if a meeting does have a purpose, its cost-effectiveness should still be considered.

Every meeting costs money. Take, for example, a meeting between a manager (total cost to the company for remuneration package at £28,000 p.a.) and a team member (total cost to the company for remuneration package at £20,000 p.a.). Assuming that the meeting lasts 1 hour and there were no travel costs:

Combined cost to the organization of employment:

£28,000 + £20,000 = £48,000

226 working days a year = 1582 hours

Cost of 1 hour meeting = £30.34

Whether it would be £30.34 well spent depends on the outcome of the meeting. If the only outcome was deciding that the office kettle should be replaced then it would be difficult to justify the cost. However, if the meeting resulted in the introduction of a more efficient rota system, then it would have been a very cost-effective use of time.

ACTIVITY 44

Select three meetings you have attended recently which involved different people. Estimate the cost to the organization for each meeting. You may need to include the cost of travelling (time and expense)

Meeting 1:

Meeting 2:

Meeting 3:

FEEDBACK

Costs are relatively easy to quantify. More difficult is making a judgment as to whether the outcomes achieved by the meeting were worthwhile – a cost-effective use of resources. People in organizations have to communicate to make things happen and often meeting face to face is the best option. Meetings can also help to build relationships which in turn can lead to improved team working, increased motivation and a better quality of decision-making.

ACTIVITY 45

For each meeting you identified in the previous activity, answer the following questions.

	Meeting 1		Meeting 2		Meeting 3	
	Yes	No	Yes	No	Yes	No
Did the outcome(s) of the meeting contribute towards meeting your work objectives?	❑	❑	❑	❑	❑	❑
Did the outcome(s) of the meeting contribute towards meeting organizational goals/targets?	❑	❑	❑	❑	❑	❑
Did everyone who was there, need to be there?	❑	❑	❑	❑	❑	❑
Were people adequately prepared so they could maximize their contribution?	❑	❑	❑	❑	❑	❑
Were discussion and contributions constructive?	❑	❑	❑	❑	❑	❑
In your judgment, was the meeting a cost-effective use of resources?	❑	❑	❑	❑	❑	❑

FEEDBACK

Before calling a meeting you need to make a judgment as to whether it will be an effective use of time. For remote teams it may be worth exploring the use of technology to avoid time spent on travelling and associated costs. For example:

- tele-conferencing/phone conversation (cheapest alternative to a face-to-face meeting)
- video-conferencing (participants can see as well as hear each other; sophisticated and costly in terms of setting up the hardware)
- Microsoft Net Meeting (a service providing data-conferencing, text chat, whiteboard and file transfer, as well as point-to-point audio and video)
- e-mail (exchanges can extend over days as ideas are circulated and conclusions reached).

There are two questions to ask before having a meeting:

1   Is this meeting necessary?   ⇒   If no   ⇒   Don't have it

  ⇓

  If yes

  ⇓

2   How can its effectiveness and efficiency be maximized?

Meeting preparation

Preparation is the key to maximizing the effectiveness and efficiency of a meeting. After identifying the purpose and outcomes of a meeting, you need to identify who should attend. You need people at a meeting who have:

- the knowledge and experience to contribute
- the skills to be constructive
- the motivation to want to see outcomes
- the authority to make decisions
- a need to be informed.

ACTIVITY 46

Select a meeting that you will be running in the near future, e.g. a regular team meeting.

- What is the purpose(s) of the meeting?

- What do you want the outcomes of the meeting to be? Try to be objective as possible.

- How long will you schedule the meeting to last?

- Is holding the meeting a cost-effective use of time and resources?

FEEDBACK

Once you've clarified the reason for holding the meeting and identified who should attend, it's essential that the other participants receive the necessary briefing. You need to distribute an agenda beforehand. For example formal agendas traditionally take the following format:

Shorebird Catering Ltd Team meeting: 02.08.04; Westland Office, 10.00 am	*Title of organization and type of meeting* *Date, time, venue*
1 Apologies for absence	*1 Apologies – a culture of receiving apologies saves time waiting for people who can't attend.*
2 Minutes of last meeting	*2 Usually these have been circulated beforehand so they can simply be approved as signed by the chair as being a true record of the last meeting.*
3 Matters arising	*3 This allows people to discuss any matters related to the last minutes, e.g. progress on actions.*

4 Main agenda:
   4.1 Christmas menu
   4.2 Staff rota
   4.3 Butcher supplies
   4.4 Customer complaints
   4.5 Staff ideas
	4 These are items which have been planned as topics to be dealt with during the meeting. Think carefully about the order. It's often best to put agenda items which need most discussion at the top.

5 Any other business (AOB)	*5 This gives the opportunity for any items which arise during the meeting to be discussed or that people have brought to the meeting but not had time to include in the main agenda.*
6 Date and time of next meeting	*6 Usually agreed during the meeting.*

Note that each agenda item is numbered.

For less formal meetings, adding detail into the agenda can help make the meeting more productive as people will be more prepared to contribute. For example:

Shorebird Catering Ltd

Team meeting: 02.08.04; Westland Office
10.00 am

1   Apologies

2   Minutes of last meeting

3   Matters arising

4   Main agenda:
    4.1 Christmas menu
        –   SD to circulate sample menus; JR to bring cover designs; LL to estimate costings

    4.2 Staff rota
        –   all to check staff holiday bookings over Christmas; maternity leave cover for HJ to be considered

    4.3 Butcher supplies
        –   action resulting from drop in quality and delivery times to be decided

    4.4 Customer complaints
        –   SD to bring latest

    4.5 Staff ideas
        –   all to collect prior to meeting

5   AOB

The agenda gives the framework for the meeting. It's useful to e-mail a draft agenda to participants to see if they want to add any agenda items. This will help you to set a realistic time limit for the meeting, based on experience.

Leading meetings

If your role is to lead a meeting, whether or not you are in the formal role of 'chair', you need to make sure that:

- all participants can contribute and that there is constructive discussion
- the agenda is followed within time constraints
- you set the framework by opening discussion, summarizing main points and ensuring action points are agreed.

It's not an easy task and involves staying in control without dominating the meeting as well as allowing all participants to be involved. Your management style will have a major impact on how you behave in a team meeting. As explored in Section 3, styles of management can be placed on a continuum from autocratic to democratic; another Theory is that managers fall into being either Theory X or Theory Y. Leading a meeting involves recognizing the importance of participation and encouraging it whilst at the same time keeping to the agenda. This will often mean that you have to stop discussion, summarize and move onto the next agenda item.

Managing a discussion

During meetings participants will discuss matters. It's easy for participants to enjoy discussing and forget the purpose of the meeting. Therefore your role is to control the discussion by:

- Introducing each agenda item clearly to give direction and remind people what they are in the meeting to do.
- Setting a time limit for a discussion.
- Keeping track of the discussion by summarizing people's input.
- Asking questions to make sure that what people have said has been understood.
- Asking participants to keep the discussion relevant – people have a habit of hijacking the agenda to make their own points.
- Making sure action points resulting from the discussion are agreed and accurately recorded. It's useful to ask the person taking the minutes to read back items, especially if they have been controversial.

Don't be afraid to interpret to keep the meeting on track. It may feel awkward but participants should respect your role in leading the meeting.

ACTIVITY 47

What communication skills are particularly relevant when you are managing a discussion?

FEEDBACK

Body language is very important. For example, facial expressions and eye contact can send clear messages in a meeting when it's time to move on or when you want to move on or summarize. You can also pick up feedback from a participant's body language as to their level of interest.

You need to speak clearly and with authority as you manage a discussion. Remember Peter Honey's research into likely responses when certain phrases are used (see Section 1).

Listening is also essential. You need to listen to what people are saying so you can summarize, clarify and ask relevant questions.

ACTIVITY 48

Select a meeting you have recently attended or led. Did you/the person leading the meeting:

	Yes	No
Keep to the agenda?	❏	❏
Introduce each point on the agenda?	❏	❏
Keep the meeting on schedule?	❏	❏
Allocate discussion time for agenda items sensibly?	❏	❏
Encourage participation?	❏	❏
Keep the discussion relevant to the agenda items?	❏	❏
Summarize at appropriate intervals?	❏	❏
Make sure action points were agreed and recorded?	❏	❏

FEEDBACK

Reflecting on other people's behaviour and reviewing your own is an important habit to get into. If you lead a meeting, ask for feedback from other participants on how it went. There's a lot you can learn from observing how other people handle situations.

Creativity in meetings

In a time-pressured work environment it's often difficult to set aside time for quality thinking time. It's often easier to pursue the most obvious, tried and tested route than to look creatively at an issue and bring in fresh ideas.

Meetings can give an opportunity to think creatively. Allowing a group of people to think laterally and generate ideas can either:

- reaffirm that the planned approach is the best one or
- introduce new approaches or methods of solving issues.

Thinking creatively is hard work. Good ideas are often the result of a lot of hard thinking or as Thomas Edison is renowned for observing:

Genius is 2 per cent inspiration and 98 per cent perspiration.

Thomas Edison

People often need to be given the space to think creatively. Meetings can be an ideal forum for giving that space in a structured way where people can bounce ideas off each other and explore new directions.

There also has to be an environment which encourages creative thinking and is receptive to it. It's within your remit as a manager to create a culture within your team which is creative.

However, the culture of an organization has a direct impact on the quality of communications. For example, in her book *The Change Masters*,[2] Kanter identified a 'segmentalist culture' in which 10 rules for stifling innovation would thrive. The same rules can apply to stifling open and honest communication.

1   Regard any new idea with suspicion – because it's new, and because it's from below.

2   Insist that people who need your approval to act first go through several other levels of management to get their signature.

3   Ask departments or individuals to challenge or criticize each other's proposals. (This saves you the task of deciding; you just pick the survivor.)

4   Express your criticisms freely and withhold your praise. (That keeps people on their toes.) Let them know they can be fired at any time.

5   Treat identification of problems as a sign of failure, to discourage people from letting you know something in their area isn't working.

6   Control everything carefully. Make sure people count anything that can be counted frequently.

7   Make decisions to reorganise or change policies in secret, and spring them on people unexpectedly. (This also keeps people on their toes.)

8   Make sure that requests for information are fully justified and make sure that it is not given out to managers freely. (You don't want data to fall into the wrong hands.)

9   Assign to lower-level managers, in the name of delegation and participation, responsibility for figuring out how to cut back, lay off, move people around or otherwise implement threatening decisions you have made. And get them to do it quickly.

10 And above all, never forget that you, the higher-ups, already know everything important about this business.

Kanter, R.M. (1983). *The Change Masters*, p. 101

ACTIVITY 49

On a continuum between encouraging innovation and stifling it, where would you place your organization.

Encouraging innovation   **Stifling innovation**

Now consider your team. On a continuum between encouraging innovation and stifling it, where would you place the predominant culture in your team?

Encouraging innovation   **Stifling innovation**

FEEDBACK

Methods you may consider using within your team include the following:

- Group thinking
- Six thinking hats
- Mind mapping.

GROUP THINKING

This is a technique which aims to unleash as many creative ideas or solutions as possible. The aim is to allow people's mind to roam free and then capture the ideas they come up with. Capturing ideas on a flipchart, however impractical or wild, can then trigger off new ideas in other people's minds which give fresh insights.

It's important that all participants are aware of the following rules:

- Every idea is valid – no matter how impractical it seems
- There should be no criticism of any idea
- Ideas mustn't be explored during the group-think session – just recorded on the flipchart. Scribe should note down every idea – no sifting
- Set a time limit, e.g. 5 minutes, but be prepared to extend if ideas are continuing to flow.

If you have a group think try and get someone other than the meeting participants to write the ideas on the flipchart. The time to discuss the ideas and select the ones which seem worthy of greater exploration is after the activity has finished.

SIX THINKING HATS

In his book *Six Thinking Hats*, de Bono[3] introduces the concept of parallel thinking. It involves looking at a problem or issue from many different angles before drawing conclusions. To do this in a systematic way de Bono introduces differently coloured 'thinking hats'. Different coloured hats can be worn in practise, although it can be enough just to have reminders of the different thinking types; e.g. on pictures on the walls, coloured squares in the centre of a central table, etc.

During a meeting, people will focus on the type of thinking associated with a particular hat. For example:

Colour of hat	Type of thinking	For instance:
White	Looking at the facts	The budget has been slashed by £50 K
Red	Identifying emotions, hunches, intuition	Anger; incredulity that the importance of the service hasn't been recognized; feeling demoralized
Black	Looking at all the problems, negative aspects	We just can't meet demand. It's not good ... because ....
Yellow	Looking at all the positive aspects	It could give us an opportunity to ...
Green	Creatively identifying ideas, solutions, actions	How about ... or...

Wearing a blue hat, the chair or team leader would take on a controlling role, asking participants to wear particular hats of categorizing contributions into a 'thinking type'.

For example:

Let's move on to focusing on green hat thinking

We seem to be dragged back into black hat thinking, can we move on to yellow hat thinking

de Bono maintains that the six hats method:

'Allows the brain to maximize its sensitivity in different directions at different times. It is simply not possible to have that maximum sensitization in different directions all at the same time'.

MIND MAPPING

Rather than starting out from the top and working down in sentence or lists, one should start from the centre with the main idea and branch out as dictated by the individual ideas and general form of the central theme.

Buzan, *Use Your Head*[4]

Tony Buzan argues that a 'mind map' better represents the way our brains make connections than the traditional linear format. During a meeting a mind map can provide a structure for identifying related issues. For example:

In a meeting a call centre team was exploring the reasons behind the increase in customer complaints. They were able to develop a mind map which captured the team's ideas on where problems lay.

Customer complaints (centre)

- Staff response
  - High turnover
  - Missing induction
  - Quality???

- Systems
  - Finance problem
  - Authority to refund

- Expectations
  - Unrealistic demands
  - Discount pricing effect
  - Time delay

If you develop a mind map in a meeting you need to:

1 identify the issue and write it in the centre
2 draw branches radiating out of the centre
3 attach relevant ideas to each of the branches.

ACTIVITY 50

Select one of the methods of encouraging creativity and consider how you would use it in a team meeting.

FEEDBACK

There are a number of barriers which can prevent creative thinking. These include:

- fear of criticism
- pressures and constraints
- not believing that you have the ability to think creatively.

However, most people respond to the invitation to look at situations creatively.

Writing the minutes

The minutes provide a record of what happened during the meeting. They ensure that everyone has the same understanding. In formal meetings a record of the main discussion points are often necessary. For example:

PORT DEVELOPMENT MEETING HELD 2nd September 2004

Venue:	Harbour Office
Present:	John Barker
	Kate Krier
	Sibina Patel
	Chris Day
Apologies:	Paul Cliffe (annual leave)

MATTERS ARISING

Caton Buoy Survey now complete (issued 29 July). This buoy is shown to mark the western boundary of a submerged bank. The shallowest part of the bank is some 500 metres east of the current buoy position. To move the buoy to the east would guard the shallowest part but would then expose the western boundary to incoming traffic.

Action: Charts to circulate to masters for comment but the view from the meeting was that it should remain in its current position.

CD – To chase
Emergency exercise. Final wash-up meeting to be scheduled for 10.10.04.

AGENDA

3.1   Dredging Consents

SB reported that all of the regulators met on the 11th April with John Eccles representing the Port of Caton. The results of this meeting were summarized in a letter stating that it is expected to determine the consent on the 20th September. Any issues raised could delay the issue of the consent.

Action: JB to check no further issues

In less formal meetings it may be decided that minutes should be in the form of action points. In this case the next meeting would begin with a review of the progress on the actions.

Team meeting – 25.11.2004

Attendees:

Noah Crossley
Keesha Bentley
Martha Smith
John Williams
Peter Mason
Frank Hindley

Summary of information, resulting agreements and actions

1   The minutes of the last meeting were read and agreed.

2   Matters arising:
    a John had explored the feasibility of contracting out.

Action: Peter to discuss with Finance Director
    b It was decided that no charge should be made for the Charter transport.

Action: Martha to inform users

It's important for any agreed actions to be clear. It is the chair's role to make sure the minutes are circulated after the meeting.

Learning summary

- Meetings can be a huge time waster. Before calling a meeting identify the cost and benefits.
- Consider alternatives such as telephone, tele-conferencing, video-conferencing.
- Always identify the purpose of a meeting.
- Prepare and circulate an agenda beforehand.
- When you lead a meeting manage the discussion, making sure people keep to the agenda.

- When leading a meeting pay particular attention to the following aspects of communication:
  - Body language
  - Listening
  - The way you speak.
- Consider using creative activities in meetings such as:
  - Group thinking
  - Six thinking hats
  - Mind mapping.
- Minutes are a record of what happened during a meeting. They ensure everyone has the same understanding and highlight action points are agreed.

Into the workplace

You need to:

- Manage meetings effectively.

References

1   Gratton, L. and Ghoshal, S. (2002) Improving the quality of conversations, *Organisational Dynamics*, 31(3), 209–223
2   Kanter, R.M. (1983) *The Change Masters*, New York, NY: Simon & Schuster
3   de Bono, E. (2004) *Six Thinking Hats*, Penguin Books Ltd
4   Buzan, T. (2003) *Use Your Head*, BBC Consumer Publishing

Section 5 Written communication

Introduction

We live in an age of 'information overload'. The ease of sending electronic documents has added to the problem. The paperless office may sound good in theory but in practice it means that people have to filter through a lot more written information to extract what they need.

It's easy to fall into the trap of thinking that anything written is about information giving. In reality, it's rarely just about information giving. In practice, it's about sending a message, which often incorporates information within it.

In this section, we look at:

- the importance of knowing what you want to achieve by writing
- how to keep it simple
- some of the drawbacks of e-mail
- writing a report.

Know your purpose

Before you start writing, you need to ask yourself:

- Who will be reading this?
- What do I want to achieve?

It's essential to be clear of your purpose and be able to capture it as a clear objective. For example, to:

- arrange a meeting
- give the results of the enquiry
- rectify the complaint.

ACTIVITY 51

Look through the last three e-mails you sent. What was the purpose of each one?

1

2

3

What was the purpose of the last three reports you have written?

1

2

3

What was the purpose of the last three letters you have written?

1

2

3

FEEDBACK

The longer the document, the easier it is to begin to drift away from achieving the purpose and added irrelevant information. You may find it useful to write your purpose on a note to refer to as you write longer documents.

Keep it simple

Most people nod sagely about the need to use plain English.

ACTIVITY 52

Read the following sentences taken from the plain English campaign website, www.plainenglishcampaign.com, and then simplify them:

1   High-quality learning environments are a necessary precondition for facilitation and enhancement of the on-going learning process. (It's referring to schoolchildren.)

2   If there are any points on which you require explanation or further particulars, we shall be glad to furnish such additional details as may be required by telephone.

FEEDBACK

The website offers the following 'translations':

1   Children need good schools, if they are to learn properly.
2   If you have any questions, please ring.

There is no doubt that people prefer to read something that is written clearly and simply than have to first interpret the words into something they can understand.

ACTIVITY 53

Why do you think that many documents written at work are unnecessarily complicated?

FEEDBACK

Deeply embedded in people's minds is that using complicated language is a mark of intelligence or seniority within an organization. It's also easier to write. The transition from ideas and thoughts into words takes a lot of processing in our brains. As we wrestle with the translation it's often easier to ramble than to be clear and succinct. Until we get into the habit, it adds another layer to the process:

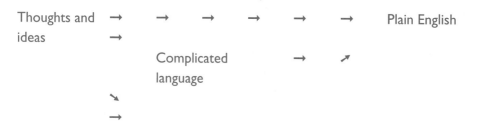

Thoughts and ⟶   ⟶   ⟶   ⟶   ⟶   ⟶   Plain English
ideas   ⟶

                       Complicated   ⟶   ↗
                       language

Inevitably, until you become skilled, writing simply will take more effort.

HOW TO WRITE CLEARLY

The five most important rules are:

1 **Keep sentences short**   There should only be *one* idea in a sentence. Try to keep the maximum number of words below twenty.
2 **Use short words which are familiar.**

ACTIVITY 54

Write down shorter, more familiar words, for the following:

commence: ascertain:

locate: in order to:

at this point in time: in the vicinity of:

make an attempt to: is not in a position to:

prior to: utilize:

terminate: consequently:

in the event of: endeavour:

You may have thought of: start, find, now, try, before, end, if, find out, to, near, can't, use, so, try.

3 **Use paragraphs**   Paragraphs help to give lengthy documents a structure. There should be only one main idea covered in one paragraph.

4 **Use bullet points or numbered lists**   Again these help to structure the document.

5 **Read it through and simplify**   When you've written something, read it with an 'editor's hat' on and simplify it. Spending time at this stage develops your skill as well as making things a lot easier for the reader.

Sending e-mails

These days the most common form of written communication you're likely to use is e-mail. Although it's hard to imagine a world without e-mail, it has its downside. For example:

- **It is overused**   The ability to 'copy' e-mails to many people has added to the problem of 'information overload'. This means that you'll often get information which you don't need; even if you don't spend time reading it, the act of filtering out what you do read takes up time.
- **Too much information is sent**   The ease at which attachments can be used means that vast quantities of information are sent. It's a technique for shifting responsibility for filtering out relevant parts from the sender to the receiver. In practice it often means that no one actually extracts the relevant information.
- **It can be an intrusion**   The arrival of an e-mail can disturb concentration. Some people find it difficult to ignore its arrival until a convenient time to deal with it.
- **It is used to avoid face-to-face communication**   The e-mails can be used to 'dump' work onto people and deliver bad news.
- **It is an easy tool for breaching confidentiality**   It's a very simple process for an employee to forward an e-mail and spread news or gossip.
- **It's easy to send by mistake**   For example '**CTRL S**' will send an e-mail and can be easily pressed instead of '**Shift S**'.

Many organizations have policies related to e-mail use. For example:

Internal e-mail policy

- In the case of urgent communications, the sender must not assume that an e-mail message has been received and if necessary must follow it up with a telephone call.
- Formal internal correspondence may be sent via e-mail, without the need for additional hard copy via conventional mail, provided that:
  - the sender's PC is set up to 'Request a read receipt' for all messages sent
  - formal e-mail correspondence and any attachments are signed with the name of the sender.
- All e-mail correspondence is 'discoverable' under the rules of evidence and can be retrieved and used in litigation, unless protected by a 'suitable rider'.
- Senders must be aware of the very large volumes of e-mail that may be received by their addressee. The 'High Importance' icon which can be attached to an e-mail to draw particular attention to it should be used only when necessary.

It's important to recognize that e-mail isn't a private communication channel:

I think that people sometimes naively believe that an e-mail is somehow not a public communication.

Chris Major, Head of PR AstraZeneca

Writing a report

A report is usually the result of an information-collection process. It's tempting to move straight into information collecting without clearly defining the following questions:

- What is the purpose of the report?
- What decisions will be made as a result of the report?

It may be useful to draft a prototype structure of a report, right at the beginning, to be sure that the information in the report will enable the decisions to be taken. For example:

Key decisions

The Corporate Management Competencies had been developed and a process created to integrate their use into performance management. Research was then required to make the following decisions:

- Should the process in its present form be cascaded throughout the company?
  - If no, what amendments should be made?
  - If yes, which methods of cascading the process should be used?

Information needed to make decisions

1 How practical and beneficial is the proposed process?
2 How practical are the following methods of cascading the information?
  - Briefings
  - One-to-one discussions between line manager and manager.

Prototype report

1 *Introduction*
  During January/February, pilot use of the management competencies in performance management was monitored on varying scales in each division such as:
  - marketing (include quantitative data for how many managers/line managers involved in each division and manner of briefing)
  - finance
  - customer response
  - etc.
2 *Summary of findings*
3 *Recommendations*
4 *Information collected*

  The following information was collected:

- The average time taken for line managers and managers to agree core competencies was x hours (include range)
- X per cent of managers/line managers found the guidance on the process of identifying core competencies to be satisfactory. The following suggestions were made for improvements:
  - yyyyyyyyyyyyyyyyyyyy (suggested by X per cent)
  - yyyyyyyyyyyyyyyyyyyy (suggested by X per cent)
  - etc.

> - X per cent of managers/line managers found the documentation to help identify core competencies to be satisfactory. The following suggestions were made for improvements:
>   - yyyyyyyyyyyyyyyyyyyy (suggested by X per cent)
>   - yyyyyyyyyyyyyyyyyyyy (suggested by X per cent)
>   - etc.
> - etc.
>
> ---
>
> Based on Backward marketing research, *Harvard Business Review*, May–June 1985, pp. 176–182.

It's highly likely that the structure of a final report will evolve. However, the discipline of thinking things through at the earliest stage can avoid time and effort being misplaced.

CONTENTS OF A REPORT

A report should be clearly divided into sections and contain the following elements:

- **A title page** (including date and name of author)
- **Contents** (if the report is longer than five pages)
- **Summary** (again if the report is longer than five pages – this should give an overview of what the report is about and the recommendations). For example, below is a summary of a review of a company's training department:

> **1   Summary**
>
> A number of factors, including feedback from customers, new corporate initiatives and the departure of the Corporate Training Officer, indicated that a comprehensive review of the Corporate Training Service (CTS) was needed. The purpose of the review was to identify potential model(s) for the future operation of the CTS.
>
> During the review, research is concentrated in four main areas:
>
> 1   Consultation with customers (details of the consultation are given in Appendix 1).
> 2   Consultation with members of staff currently involved in the delivery of training (details are given in Appendix 2).
> 3   Review of planned corporate initiatives which involves changes in employees' skills, behaviours or attitudes.
> 4   Investigation of external good practice which could influence the structure and delivery mechanisms used.

Analysis of the information obtained resulted in two potential models for a revised CTS:

- **Option 1** Strengthened CTS
- **Option 2** Minor amendments to current CTS (a description of the existing CTS is given in Appendix 3).

These options are described in detail in the report. After each description the rationale behind it is given with a summary of any potential pitfalls and funding implications:

- A third potential option (Appendix 4) involves centralizing all training and training budgets, as well as increasing the number of corporate training personnel significantly. This has been dismissed as being impractical within the current structures of the company.

Recommendations

Option 1 (Section 3) should be selected.

The schedule for the appointment of the main post (Corporate Training Consultant) to support option 1 is as follows:

The summary should give an overview of what's in the report and its recommendations:

- **Introduction** This should include the purpose of the report and its terms of reference.
- **Main body of the report** This should be clearly structured into numbered paragraphs.
- **Conclusion** These are the main findings of the report and must be based on the information in the main body of the report.
- **Recommendations** These include the recommended actions and must clearly result from the conclusions.
- **Appendices** These should give information about what was used in the report.

Always write the main body of your report before attempting the summary, conclusions or recommendations.

It's vital that you keep your reader in mind when writing a report. They need a clear structured route to the conclusions and recommendations.

ACTIVITY 55

Compare four reports written by different people in your organization. Which report do you consider to be the most effective in meeting its purpose. Why?

FEEDBACK

Assessing reports other people have written is a useful way of developing your own skills. Identifying how they could have been improved can help you make sure that you don't make the same mistakes.

Learning summary

- When you write you need to communicate, not just send information.
- Before you start writing you need to ask yourself:
    - Who will be reading this?
    - What do I want to achieve?
- To write clearly:
    - keep sentences short
    - use short words which are familiar
    - use paragraphs
    - use bullet points of numbered lists
    - read it through and simplify.
- Remember that e-mails have disadvantages – i.e. it's not a private communication channel.
- Think through the *content* of a report before you start any work collecting information.

- A report can be divided into the following main elements:
  - A title page
  - Contents
  - Summary
  - Introduction
  - Main body of the report
  - Conclusions
  - Recommendations
  - Appendices.

Into the workplace

You need to:

- Write in plain English
- Use e-mail with caution
- Structure a report.

Information toolbox

Communication skills

Berne, E. (1964) *Games People Play*, Penguin

Goleman, D. (1996) *Emotional Intelligence*, Bloomsbury

Heyman, R. (1997) *Why Didn't You Say That in the First Place?* Jossey-Bass Publishers

Holtz, S. (2004) *Corporate Conversations*, Amacom

Honey, P. (1997) *Improve Your People Skills*, IPD

Langford-Wood, N. and Salter, B. (2002) *Critical Corporate Communications*, CBI

Ma, D. (1998) *One Stop Communication*, ICSA Publishing

Theobald, T. and Cooper, C. (2004) *Shut Up and Listen!* Kogan Page

Cultures and communication

Guirdham, M. (1999) *Communicating Across Cultures*, Ichor Business Books

Presentations/briefings

Hind, T. (1998) *Making Presentations*, Dorling Kindersley

The Industrial Society (June 2000) *Team Communications – Managing Best Practice* Series

Meetings

Dobson, A. (1996) *Managing Meetings*, How To Books Ltd, Plymbridge House

Hindley, T. (1998) *Managing Meetings*, Dorling Kindersley

Writing in plain English

www.plainenglishcampaign.com This website offers free guidelines on writing in plain English as well as a variety of packs of materials and training.

CMI Management Information Centre

One of the benefits of membership of the Chartered Management Institute is free and unlimited access to a library containing more than 30 000 books and 40 000 articles. The Institute provides tailored reading lists on any management topic requested. These are usually e-mailed to you on the same day as you request them. All books and articles are posted first class and are therefore received the day after ordering.

Telephone: 01536 207307   Website: www.managers.org.uk

RELEVANT CMI CHECKLISTS

Checklist 002 Handling effective meetings
Checklist 031 Effective communications: delivering presentations
Checklist 032 Effective communications: planning presentations
Checklist 051 Report writing.